Would You Like to Be a Catholic?
EUGENE KENNEDY

ST. ANTHONY MESSENGER PRESS

Cincinnati, Ohio

Cover and book design by Mark Sullivan
Dedication page illustration by Ron Bailey

Library of Congress Cataloging-in-Publication Data
Kennedy, Eugene C.
  Would you like to be a Catholic? / Eugene Kennedy.
    p. cm.
  ISBN 0-86716-530-8 (alk. paper)
  1. Catholic Church—Doctrines. I. Title.
  BX1751.3.K46 2003
  282—dc22

                                              2003015380

ISBN 0–86716–530–8
Published by St. Anthony Messenger Press
www.AmericanCatholic.org
Printed in the U.S.A.

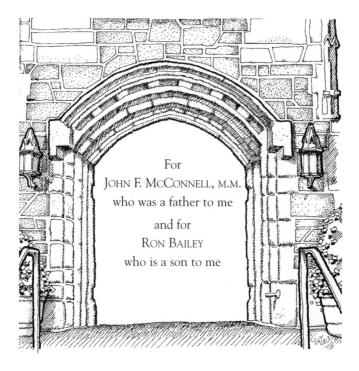

For
JOHN F. McCONNELL, M.M.
who was a father to me

and for
RON BAILEY
who is a son to me

CONTENTS

CHAPTER ONE

Did You Ever Want to Belong to a Big Family?

What is it like to be a Catholic? What is it really like and just where would we go to find out?

Sometimes, even Catholics must admit, their religion seems more like a pageant or a front-page story than it does a Church.

When high-spirited young believers from around the world sing in the presence of a smiling pope, Catholics make us wonder what their secret is and perhaps even to long for a share of their unaffected joy for ourselves. When preoccupied cardinals from America ponder priests who sexually abuse children before a frowning Holy Father, Catholics make us wonder about something that is surprising about them, that they hold onto their faith even when their leaders break faith with them.

1

What is it about being a Catholic that, as welcome as a coastal light to a lost sailor, seems to fill these believers with hope in the darkest of nights and opens them to joy at dawn? How is it that Catholics can define sin clearly and yet never seem to be surprised by it and are always ready to forgive it? What is it that lines them up on the side of life, as in the pro-life movement, and sets the teeth of the popular culture on edge? The latter leaves not so much as an inch of space uncovered by its billboards advertising the modern age's preferred version of morality as consumer behavior, as personal and private as a shopping excursion in which the array of goods is infinite. Take what you want, it says, because *choice* is our household god, *choice* is a right more than a duty, and *making the choice* is the moral action and *what you choose* is no big deal.

How can Catholics stand up to and challenge this accepted modern design in which self soars at the center of life as enigmatic and indifferent to its surroundings as the Egyptian obelisk in St. Peter's Square? What is it about what they believe that makes Catholics reject what so many others accept—the notion that morality is our own business and that we measure it by our own needs and feelings? And isn't that why we have a Supreme Court, to tell us what is right and wrong and to defend the sanctuary of our privacy?

What is it about these Catholics, even in the bad times when they learn that so many priests, and even some bishops, are guilty of sexually abusing children and then covering it up, making the whole Church into a virtual crime scene? They react like the family that they claim to be and, for all its faults, they seem to love their Church and, like a good family, they stick together in good times and bad.

Catholicism certainly stands out in bad times, such as those terrible days after the September 11 terrorist attacks. The Catholic Church preaches eternal life but also has a jeweler's case of the right symbols for our lives right now. Its signs and rites are a special language that speak to our human need for symbols of our loss and our longing in a way that touches something deep even in the religiously estranged or unChurched onlookers. It silences the commentators who can neither add to nor subtract from these simple public spiritual transactions that break us briefly free of time's grip so that we all get a whiff of the eternal from the same updraft of the spirit that seems to fill Catholics with a peace that really is beyond understanding.

What is going on in this great old vessel of a Church that Catholics refuse to abandon it even as it takes on water from ramming into a sex abuse scandal that seemed to confirm the worst of the centuries of heavy shelling by its critics? What keeps these Catholics calm, aware of, but unshaken by, the apparent confusion among its officers about what to do next? Why are they so peaceful instead of starting a mutiny or swamping the lifeboats?

The bad beginning of the twenty-first century for the Catholic Church is actually a good time to learn about Catholics. We know that the whole story is never found in the headlines and, as far as the Catholic Church is concerned, seldom in the editorials of *The New York Times* or *The Washington Post*, either. We also understand that neither the high nor the low points in anybody's life tell the truth, the whole truth and nothing but the truth about them. Like a storm skinning the insulation from a wire, bad news exposes something about all of us, but, *there's more to us than that*, we say, *you need to find out more about us before you make up your minds about us*. So, if we recycle the newspapers and drape dust sheets on the televisions and the computers, how would we find out *more* that is trustworthy about Catholics and about their Church?

We might enter a library as quiet as a cathedral and survey the teachings of the Catholic Church in its official catechism. Undistracted by the parade of the living Church passing by outside—it will still be going by when the library closes—we could review the documents of the Second Vatican Council (1962–1965). There we would find the story of how the bishops of the world—working with the first among them, the bishop of Rome who is thereby the pope—renewed and revitalized Catholic teachings, updating them in the language of the times and revealing the depths of their relevance to the modern world. We could also consult many books about the Church, such as theologian Richard McBrien's *Catholicism*, that present Catholic teachings in a clear and highly readable manner.

Examined in a library alcove, the Catholic Church, because its story is long and vivid, colorful and complicated, might appear, on the one hand, to be the *Masterpiece Theater* of churches, renewed every season with a wise and elderly moderator who not only gives continuity to the varied series but a sense of aren't-we-wise-to-tune-in even though not all the tales intrigue us. On the other hand, Catholicism might, in columnist Jimmy Breslin's phrase, come across as the Marine Corps of churches, so tough on recruits and demanding in its rules that its motto is, quite rightly, *Semper Fidelis*, always faithful.

If partial, prejudiced and highly personal impressions arise from such sources, the best way to find out about the Catholic Church turns out to be the ideal way to find out about anything or anybody. We need to meet Catholics in person to learn for ourselves what they are like and what it is about them and their Church that makes us wonder about them.

The Catholic Church has been through many bad times and the siege of the sex abuse scandal has given Catholics an unexpected public test of what they are like. In bad times, of course, people tell us what they really think. So, if the best revelation of Catholicism is found in the lives of ordinary Catholics, a wonderful opportunity to mingle with them and to take their measure arose during the long, harsh early season of disclosures of sex abuse by some of their priests and, even worse, attempts to cover it up by some of their bishops.

If many Catholic officials looked bad during these long months of inquiry, ordinary Catholics looked good. While pundits gave learned opinions on the problem, average Catholics spoke for themselves, in impromptu interviews outside their parish Churches. They responded with some of the anger, hurt and tears that reporters sought as offerings to the gods of eye-witness news, but these Catholics also did something that made the television eye blink in surprise.

Almost every one of them—from older ladies making their way cautiously down cathedral steps to Boomer couples shep-herding their children into their SUVs after Mass to the blue collar workers coming out the side door arm-in-arm with wives bearing beehive hairdos—gave the same answer when they were asked about their attitude toward the sex abuse scandal in the Church.

These garden-variety Catholics gave the world an unre-hearsed theology lesson about the nature of their Church and their membership in it. They made a clear, crucial and accurate distinction between Catholicism as a religious faith and Catholicism as a human organization. Their faith in Catholicism as a religion remained strong despite the unfolding scandal but their confidence in the leaders of institutional Catholicism suffered greatly because of the latter's mismanage-ment of, and efforts to cover up, the problem. This was a crisis of the Church as an all-too-human institution rather than of the Church as their spiritual home. As naturally as they defined themselves as American citizens, these everyday Catholics offered to a curious world a description of the Church that the-ologians would endorse and the pope would applaud.

We know that we are the Church, they responded, revealing a consciousness of the nature of Catholicism that a thousand the-ological lectures could not explain and a million-dollar public relations campaign could never deliver. The Church will survive because it isn't the bishops and it isn't the buildings, it's us, a People of God and, after we purify it, we will nourish its life as it nourishes our own.

These Catholics and their Church, this *family,* as they call it, are not understood easily for they seem to contradict so much that we have heard about them. Mistrust them and their Church, denounce them both—some people have made their life's work out of this. And we have known people who have entered the Church and others who have left it, each of them for reasons we wish we knew, for they make us even more curious about what it is like to be a Catholic.

Would we like to be Catholic? Beneath the everyday din of modern life, let us first carve out a quiet space in which to learn more about it....

Catholicism, as described by the media, is a vast and forbidding entity with a memory that matches its rich inventory of traditions, rules and rituals, not to mention intrigues (rumored or real) for every occasion. Catholics, however, do not experience, characterize or, often enough, even recognize their Church in these quick media sketches. For them, it is not a secret society with passwords that convey a sense of social privilege. Neither do they enter it with the resignation or dread many people carry with them into the vast bland institutional hives of their daily labor in big business, the law, higher education or the postal service. Don't mistake the finely grinding mills of its bureaucracy for the real Church, they say, and don't believe everything you read about it.

Even when Catholics are displeased with some actions of their bishops—the men who are Catholicism's leaders—they make careful distinctions between these men who wear the miters of institutional authority and the Church as they themselves experience it. To describe that, most Catholics use words of easy and safe intimacy. They regard their Church not as a powerhouse but an extended family, not a labyrinth of controlled movement but a home in which they feel safe and, in no need of defenses, can be themselves.

We are the Church, they attest simply; *we* are the Church. They know in their bones what Vatican Council II, drawing on traditional and orthodox understandings, affirms: that the Church is, first and foremost, a People of God. Everything else—the buildings, the bishops, and the buzzing officials—are in place to serve this people, not to dominate them or to turn their spiritual pilgrimage into a middle passage to a cruel destiny of submission. These Catholics on the street have it right. The very word *administration*, from the Latin *ad ministrare*, means "to be of service to" rather than "in control of."

These average Catholics also show that they are comfortable with a central religious term that comes only haltingly to the lips of some of their Church's administrators. They are at ease with the Church as a people involved in the *Mystery* of salvation, that is, the saving work of Jesus in history. Catholicism is not the worship of a distant God by a servile people who turn their faces away out of fear of beholding that face and seeing into those fierce eyes. Catholicism is religion up close and always personal. Fundamentally a Mystery of human relationships, Catholicism is a way of experiencing intimacy with God through their relationships with each other.

VATICAN II AND THE PEOPLE OF GOD

This remarkable reality was emphasized by the bishops of the world when, in and through their relationships with each other and with the pope as the bishop of Rome, they spoke of the Church at Vatican Council II as a *People of God*, devoting an entire chapter to it in one of that council's principal documents, the Dogmatic Constitution on the Church *(Lumen Gentium)*. Not only did they choose the *People of God* as their principal image of the Church, but they placed its discussion in a chapter that emphasizes its profoundly human characteristics. This metaphor of the Church as a People is the blueprint; the structures are the scaffolding that may be peeled away when the cathedral is finished. So this chapter that celebrates the Church as a People, as the blueprint that breathes its spirit, is found ahead of the chapter on the Church and its organizational structures, to emphasize that, as theologian Richard McBrien explains it, "the Church is a community with a hierarchical structure rather than a hierarchical body with spiritual subjects."[1]

CHAPTER TWO

What Is Religion and Why Have a Church?

If you have ever wondered about being a Catholic, you may already have asked these questions of yourself and the great world about you. Most of us have had the answers handed (or handed down) to us before we were even curious about these issues. We inherit our ideas about what religion is and why we belong to a Church along with the family Bible and the family photo album.

It is natural, however, for people one day to open the boxes they stored away unwrapped after the will was read and to judge for themselves what elements of their inheritance they want to keep—and what they want to throw out. As they decide what silver and china they will use in the future, they may also reevaluate their spiritual beliefs and practices. They may nod and pass to the next item on the list or they may pause to examine their religious endowment. Measuring it against their own life experience, they either store it away again or remove the contents, dust them off and decide to make better use of them in the future.

Still others of us make a checkmark on our list of shipments from the past, appreciating our religious heritage as though it were the venerable grandfather clock with the wonderful insides: we'd wanted it since childhood, but now are not at all sure we want it or even know what to do with it. It is handsome and it chimes regularly, and—don't get us wrong—we like it well enough and will hand it down to our children, too. It was magnificent and mysterious when we were children, but it's part of the furniture now and, although it stands guard in the background of many family pictures, it has lost its enchantment and we would never think to set our watches by it.

DIALING THE DIVINE 911

Most of us do inherit our religion and our Churches, too, but we never think to set our lives by them. We remember them when somebody is sick or the times are bad, or, on occasion, as we shall see, we use religion like a casino chip, making a bet or a bargain as we place it on the red or the black of our needs or anxieties, *If you get me a job, or make me well again, I'll go to Church every Sunday....*

God hears a lot of these wagers every day, of course, on everything from our most profound personal problems to our hope that God will help the home team win. We sometimes file our promise in a well-thumbed mental folder of forgotten pledges and are thankful that God does not engage a collection agency to call in these promissory notes. There is something touching about the way we humans turn to God the way children do to a father who never tires of the questions beyond counting.

These bargains—*If you do this, I'll do that*—are footnotes to faith that are found in all our lives and they help us understand that, even if we inherit our religion and our Church, our hymnal and our pew, we must grow in our understanding of ourselves and our faith if we are ever to make them our own. Such negotiating with God, much like regarding a parent as magical, reflects a stage in our overall spiritual growth. This development is a living process rather than a lesson memorized to pass the Judgment Day finals. Every one of its elements—the believer, the beliefs and the Church—have meaning only in and through living personal relationships.

THE IDEA OF RELIGION

Religion is sometimes relegated to a corner of life or dealt with as if it were some large amiable pet—a part of nature and a part of us, too, but sometimes retrieving a boot instead of a bird and hard to keep out of the house no matter what we say. Culturally, we try to domesticate religion, saving it a place at civic banquets or a chair at Fourth of July celebrations, but forbidding it to cross the double yellow line painted down the middle of the nation's daily business. Except, of course, in an emergency, when we wave it over, come-as-you-are and hold our hands when terrorists strike or a space shuttle explodes in the morning sky.

We can think of religion as a consumer good, *Follow directions for adult dosage. Principal side effect: obsessiveness, occasional superstition.* That is a pragmatic use of religion as a cure, an answer or a comfort. But is religion summed up as a second cousin to the placebo effect, that improvement in our sense of well-being generated by sugar pills?

Religion is tougher, stronger and more humanly demanding than any of these representations. It is traced to such words of origin as *relegere*, "to turn to constantly" or "to observe conscientiously"; *re eligere*, "to choose again"; and *re ligare*, "to bind oneself back,"[2] or "to reconnect." *Religio*, from the old French and the Latin, refers to the "bond between man and the gods."[3] It carries as its seed the notion of a relationship, the establishment of a connection, that is, something in which we are not merely acted upon but in which are actively involved. We are agents in relationship. No surrogate acts on our behalf. The nature and outcome of the relationship depend on how, and how much, of our true selves we give to it.

For the great Doctor of the Roman Catholic Church, Saint Thomas Aquinas, religion "denotes properly a relation to God."[4] Just as we fail in human relationships if we give only a portion of ourselves to them, so the relationship we call *religion* fails if we invest only part of ourselves, or on a part-time basis, or only when we need a favor or a deliverance. Those are the signs of an immature relationship—a child's relationship. We must grow through these, "put away the things of a child," as Saint Paul expresses it, to achieve an adult relationship with God.

Centuries after Aquinas, in his classic work *The Varieties of Religious Experience*, philosopher William James described religion as "a man's total reaction upon life."[5] This catches the flavor of the Catholic theologian's understanding that religion "has to do with the whole of human existence." Religion is never fully expressed, therefore, by a part of us or on a part-time basis.

Religion may be understood as "the whole complex of attitudes, convictions, emotions, gestures, rituals, beliefs, and institutions by which we come to terms with and express, our most fundamental relationships with Reality (God and the Created order, perceived as coming forth from God's creative hand)."[6] Catholics are very clear about how this sense of creation is disclosed through God's self-revelation to us. Through religion, however, we are not just passively filled to overflowing by this revelation.

In the Catholic understanding of religion we "deliberately reach out toward" the God whom we perceive sacramentally, that is, in the persons, occurrences, events and things that we see. This sacramental sense of the world, of God's perpetual self-disclosure through creation, is both the foundation and the keystone of the Catholic understanding of religion. It is a response to all of creation by all of us. That is why religion in general, and Catholicism in particular, does not reject but embraces the human, with whose imperfect glories it is completely comfortable.

Religion is, therefore, our response in a hundred human ways, through art and story and prayer and song, but just as much through the longings we feel deeply within us at the return of spring, or in the small signals of love transmitted through eyes and embraces that are as powerful as the large signals of God's inexhaustible revelation. Everything human counts in Catholicism, everything created bears the genetic code of its Creator. Churches are formed, as we shall see, into human institutions, that is, structures that reflect and match our human nature and needs. The function of these institutions is to remember and sing the truths of creation to the created world, in ritual and symbol, in sacrament and celebration. Before, however, we explore the meaning of *Church* as in *Catholic Church*, we may look more deeply at how religion, a phenomenon that also fits our natures, can reflect, in its forms, the varying stages of our own growth to adulthood.

RELIGION AS HYPOCRISY/HYPOCRISY AS RELIGION

Everybody knows people who sing God's praises in Church on Sunday morning but, immediately afterward, hang up their beliefs with their best clothes (*That takes care of that for another week*). They neither permit nor encourage—indeed they never think of the possibility of—any overflow of the Sabbath religion's influencing the way they treat their families, friends or employees during the work week. Observing the disconnection between the way some believers claim to love God while not much liking their neighbors, certain people write such religion off as camouflage for hypocrites and want nothing to do with it.

These people are not reacting to fully developed religion but rather to half-grown or stunted religion, faith that is not faith at all. There is a lot of this going around, as they say of a flu that gives everybody the same symptoms. What are the symptoms shared by such cavalier Churchgoers and wouldn't we be better off staying away from any Church that lets them in?

We should note that this superficial profession of faith may be observed in every continent and in every form of religion. That is how zealots can praise their maker at dawn and blow up a school bus before lunch. So demanding is real religion on equating what we believe with how we behave that it has often been misunderstood and misused by people who regard faith as a play, a make-believe in one act a week in which they recite, but need not mean, their lines. Indeed, the word *hypocrite* comes from the Greek word for *actor*, one who speaks words written by another.

True religion cannot coexist with hypocrisy, the original cover-up, the sin-as-pious-disguise that is repeatedly condemned by Jesus Christ in the Gospels. He speaks of those who may have God's name on their lips while their hearts are far away and of the superficially religious who enlarge the religious symbols on their clothing to seem godly to others. The truly religious person, however, is the widow slipping her mite quietly out of her sleeve and into the collection basket or the man standing in the shadows near the back of the temple, whose deepest spiritual realization is also his simplest prayer—that he is a sinner in need of God's mercy.

Hypocrisy has a history as long as that of religion and, feeding off it like a parasite, it nourishes only itself. No hypocrites need apply for membership in a religion like Catholicism that insists that belief and behavior be integrated, that they form a whole rather than parts forced together despite their lack of fit. People who fit together are said to possess integrity. In the Catholic spiritual tradition this integrity or wholeness is the basic definition of holiness. Both holiness and wholeness derive from the old English root *hal* that means "health." These concepts, as we shall see, cannot be split apart in the Catholic understanding of faith without destroying that faith.

RELIGION MATURE AND IMMATURE - article

If health, wholeness, and holiness are not an alien wafer of veneer but the deepest grain in the wood of Catholic belief, we may borrow a distinction from religious psychology to differentiate surface religion from profound faith. Harvard psychologist Gordon Allport first introduced the distinction between mature, or *intrinsic*, faith and immature, or *extrinsic*, faith more than half a century ago.[7] It has proven to be an enduring and fruitful way to discriminate between the ways that we may profess religious faith.

Allport was attracted to the issue after observing that, as in our earlier example, the faith of some regular Sunday Churchgoers had little, if any, impact on their behavior during the rest of the week. He was puzzled by Churchgoers who could espouse religion and racial prejudice at the same time. Such persons appeared to experience no discomfort at holding viewpoints incompatible with the general religious judgment that loving God and hating our brothers and sisters were mutually exclusive positions. How could so many people fail to evince even a twinge of conscience at professing a faith that preached love for all while giving safe harbor within themselves to prejudice that prescribed hatred for certain groups?

Allport developed a scale to measure what he termed *intrinsic* versus *extrinsic* religion. As we have observed, we all inherit a religion of some kind from our parents. At first we don it much as we do the clothes that they choose for us as children. We fulfill the external demands of inherited religion—attendance at Church, reading the Bible, observing religious feasts and holidays—much as we fulfill the external demands of family tradition—going to Yale or Notre Dame, becoming a lawyer or a longshoreman, showing up at family weddings and wakes. These are social responses to which, to some extent, we are conditioned and which we accept on the generalized attribution of authority that we give to Church elders or family ancestors. At a certain time in life, Allport suggested, we examine these values that we have previously accepted without qualm or question. This may occur at a moment of change (entering college), or a moment of crisis (an illness or death), or at a moment of unexpected self-exploration (in falling in love or becoming disillusioned with a career).

Whatever the occasion, these are the times people ask questions about matters that they had previously accepted because, *Well, that's the way things have always been in our family,* that is what we have always believed, that is what we have always done. They now compare what they had accepted as adequate symbols for, and interpretations of, their lives with their own subjective sense of that same experience. *I am in law school,* they say, *because everybody in our family has always been a lawyer, being a lawyer is what is expected of me*—but *being in law school does not satisfy me, being a lawyer does not excite me, why am I doing this anyway?*

TO BE OR NOT TO BE

We have reached the divide in the road where Hamlet contemplates the choice that Robert Frost says makes "all the difference." Now we either reject the tradition in which we can no longer invest ourselves to honor our forebears—or the religion we can no longer believe in because our forefathers did. Or we can search the experience that has brought us to this moment to find motives to accept this tradition or profess this faith for reasons of our own. We assess a career or a faith we have previously accepted on somebody else's word—an *extrinsic* commitment—and we either cast it aside or, for reasons we discover in ourselves, make it our own, that is, internalize it so that it becomes an *intrinsic* commitment on our part.

Allport explains that the persistence of prejudiced behavior by avowedly religious persons may be understood through this distinction between extrinsic faith and intrinsic faith. Extrinsic faith, concerned with memory and surfaces, can coexist with racial prejudice but intrinsic faith, concerned with the present and with the depths of moral choice, cannot. His insights help us understand the pointed differences between people whose faith may be termed *extrinsic* and those whose faith may be described as *intrinsic*.

Extrinsic, or *immature*, faith accepted on the authority of others, rules out any questions but readily gives answers to every religious doubt or inquiry and is not applied to business or life choices. Intrinsic, or *mature*, faith accepted on the basis of personal experience and conviction, does not give easy answers but rather asks more questions and is routinely and systematically applied to all professional and personal choices. Indeed, intrinsic religion is identified as a *master motive* in the lives of those who profess it; it is their moral compass in locating true north and in locating their position on all important matters in life. As a thoroughly internalized belief system, it permeates the person because it is integrated into, rather than grafted onto, the personality of the believer.

One cannot be seriously interested in any religion for only socially acceptable or superficial reasons. To choose again as an adult—and in an adult manner—explains Hamlet's question, *the* religious question of all time: Are we *to be* or *not to be*, to be for ourselves what we have previously been only for the sake of others? It is the perennial spiritual challenge and, although it may be agonizing to ask the question, discovering the answer is a necessary and transforming process. We achieve our *whole-ness*—our *integrity*—as believers and persons through just such a process. This is an intensely personal journey. Nobody can make it for us. To be or not to be, that *is* the question. We cannot achieve wholeness, health or holiness without answering it.

DO WE REALLY NEED A CHURCH?

People may concede their spiritual natures and their spiritual needs but still ask: Do we really need a Church through which to experience or to express these? Even granting that the finest human ideas and causes run like protoplasm or uncooked pudding unless they are poured into forms that identify and shape their strength—the river's power is wild until it is dammed to nourish the fields and turn on the lights in the valley—many people, especially Americans, remain suspicious of institutions in general and of institutional Churches in particular. They point to the religious wars whose battle smoke, like the light from distant stars, floats back endlessly to us from long ago, obscuring the "religious" reasons that moved men to murder then and raising a blood-spattered shield over men's motives for killing in the name of God or Allah now.

That organized religion has been used to focus hatred and divisions throughout history illustrates the distorted effects of *extrinsic* faith that employs religion as an instrument of corrupted power rather than as a medium of healthy authority. We have also seen the power line language of religion dragged down and shorted out so that it does not disturb the darkness because it no longer lights the world. When, as we will discuss later, a spiritual metaphor, such as *The Promised Land*, is mistranslated into a hard geographical survey, it chops up the territory into trench warfare in which the lines taken, yielded, and retaken, finally overlap themselves to hang on the world like a barbed wire wreath of loss and death.

Would we not be better off, some have asked (great figures among them) if we worshiped God in our hearts rather than within the stifling and possibly destructive confines of an institutional structure? The founding fathers of America favored a vague *Deism* by which an even vaguer God kicked the universe into motion and then lost interest in it. Every other generation rebels against its cultural institutions, denying their value and proposing a life without them. The vessel of marriage, for example, has been set afire and sent out to sea while the mutineers, thinking they have discovered a new continent, land where men have beached throughout history, on a "natural" world in which men and women live in everlasting bliss and innocence because they have never been yoked with such institutional commitments as marriage. That relic, the self-congratulating rebels claim, is "only a piece of paper" that, in the flaming wreckage of the good ship marriage, curled up into flecks scattered like men's ashes by the four winds.

ARE INSTITUTIONS GOOD OR BAD FOR HUMAN NATURE?

The bill comes due on all rebellions that misread human nature. So now, the long-term effects of couples living together outside the institution of marriage are being calculated. The human cost is higher than its advocates ever imagined. This seemingly "free" arrangement does not prepare couples for the maturing pledge that is demanded by marriage and, instead of improving their relationship, appears, on the basis of cross-cultural studies, to compromise their chances for long-term stability and happiness.

Living together without accepting and entering the institution of marriage, with its demands for fidelity and its flowering into new lives and new responsibilities, along with its alternating seasons of better and worse, sickness and health, does not seem to fit or serve men and women nearly as well as the relationship guided and strengthened by the institution. Marriage symbolizes and supplies something that men and women need to live successfully together. Not the least dimension of this is the imperative to change internally themselves, to grow for the sake of the marriage, that is, for the sake of each other. So, too, we may say that, despite the excesses of misbegotten religious-like institutions and the claims that, left alone, men would make cathedrals of themselves, a Church as a symbol and source of spiritual life for a community responds to human needs and to human depths. How is a man, or a woman, born again? By undergoing the birth pangs of their better selves as they come to life in relationship to each other with the support and guidance of many institutions, including their Church.

The family, which grows out of marriage, is a durable institution, tested by time and evolutionary processes, and is the ideal environment for the growth of human beings. They thrive in the family as they do in no other arrangement that seeks to supplant it or to make up for its absence. So, too, a Church builds on and serves spiritually men and women in their relationship to God through their relationship with each other and with their communities. Christianity reveals its essential meaning as a special family whose function is not the arbitrary control of its members but the well-ordered flourishing of men and women as fully human, fully whole and, therefore, truly spiritual persons.

YES, BUT WHO NEEDS A CHURCH?

Individualistic Catholicism is the religious oxymoron of all time. Americans romanticize loners who arrive mysteriously in a town, like Shane in the classic Western movie, or Rick in *Casablanca*, where they reluctantly, not to say truculently, perform heroic deeds and then leave, rejecting any ongoing relationship with the town they have delivered and, of course, marriage to the beautiful woman they have saved. This is not the *ugly* but the *institutionless* American, riding or striding away, his duty done and to hell with it, his gruff independence intact. This American dream is a fantasy that does not work in real life, is incompatible with Christian teaching and gives rise to bestsellers like *Bowling Alone* that surprise the nation by tracking the epidemic loneliness and isolation of so many of its citizens. We cannot be or become Catholics on our own or live as Catholics by ourselves with the noise of the world well shut out.

The Church exists not to make us serve it but to serve our most profound human needs. Every human need or aspiration possesses a spiritual lining. Everything we say or do casts a spiritual shadow and the Church exists as an organization and an institution to catch these and to symbolize and to celebrate the human pilgrimage, spiritual at every step and choice point, throughout life. The Church does not exist for itself but for us, the men and women who lead their lives in communion with it through communion with each other. Reference books define a Church as "a company of all Christians regarded as a mystical spiritual body,"[8] and only secondarily as a building or physical structure.

A BIG NOISY FAMILY

Indeed, the Greek origin is found in *Kuriakos*, meaning "of the Lord," and the root of this word reveals the richness of the concept. It comes from a stub that means a "hollowed-out place" and is related to a "swell" or a "wave," that is, a phenomenon that by its nature grows from within itself before our eyes. The root identifies the Church as a place set aside for growth, an environment in which human spiritual growth—a three word phrase that describes a seamless process—is encouraged and supported by its community, its ministers and by its store of symbols and sacraments.

If the Church means a place of growth *in* and *of* the Lord, then it is right, as we read in the earliest commentaries by theologians termed "Church Fathers," to understand Catholicism as a family, a big one, and often noisy, as all healthy families are. Catholicism is not only a family in itself but it also constitutes a family of Churches.

Family is a metaphor, that is, a special way of speaking about reality that reveals layers of richness and meaning that are not communicated by concrete everyday language or by such other languages as mathematics or the many dialects of the computer. *Metaphor* and *myth* are the native tongues of all religions. We employ *metaphors* (from the Greek *meta*—meaning "beyond" or "after"; and *phorein*—"to bear") to "carry us beyond," to allow us to make journeys of understanding unavailable through more prosaic language. We employ myth (from the Greek *mythos* for "story") to tell our most important human stories, those that tell us who we are. Myth is the form that protects these deepest truths against the ravages of time and chance that attack other ways of describing our worlds, such as the fine columns of facts and figures in encyclopedias and almanacs that go out of date as soon as they are composed.

STOP SIGNS AND SACRAMENTS

What is important in metaphors is their spiritual rather than their literal significance. The stop sign at the corner is very literal. Its denotation is as simple and uncomplicated as it must be to accomplish its purpose. The meaning of a metaphor, on the other hand, is found in its connotation, in its capacity to bear meanings deeper than those that are strictly literal. We will return to these notions later but for now we accept the metaphor of a family, not for its literal denotation but for its rich connotations. We cannot plumb the spiritual meaning of a Church unless we make the pilgrimage into its spiritual depths by way of our principal metaphor of the family.

In Hebrew, the term for family is *bet ab*, "Father's House." In patriarchal times, this term bulged like a sail above a crowded vessel on the Nile. Waved cheerfully aboard was a very large household that included the husband and father, the wife or wives as well as the concubines, along with children, slaves, retainers, clients, the widowed and the unmarried, and, in notions that resonate even in post-modern times, those termed resident aliens, expelled daughters and unmarried adult sons and daughters. We remember that, for the Jews, the family was a religious unit and so the Passover, then as now, was celebrated within the family.[9]

A family makes room for everybody. Indeed, so, too, does a Church and as contemporary Catholics reflexively call the Church their family, so the earliest followers of Jesus regarded it in the same way. In the late fourth century Saint John Chrysostom, commenting on the book of Genesis, called the family the *ekklesia*, the Church. More recently, Pope Leo XIII, writing of Christian marriage, observed that the family was "the first form of the Church on this earth." This metaphor is affirmed in the documents of Vatican Council II (1962–1965) as well. In the *Constitution on the Church in the Modern World* the family is called "the domestic Church" (#11) and the "Christian family" is described as showing "forth to all...the authentic nature of the Church" (#48). In its document on the role of lay people, Vatican II refers to the family as the "domestic sanctuary" (#11). Even *monsignor*, the honorific conferred on certain Catholic clergy and the butt of as much ironic humor as it is the shield of ecclesiastical achievement, originates in the idea of one who serves the family or the household of the Lord. Thus, the title *monsignor*, which means "domestic prelate," is a footnote in the history of the Church as a family.

NOT A SENTIMENTAL JOURNEY

It is not, therefore, sentimental to describe the Church as a family. We cannot otherwise grasp its spiritual reality and its central theme of being a community in whose everyday life the principle of mediation is a significant dynamism. Life in a family is mediated, first through the relationship of the parents with each other and with their children, and every day, as the family gathers for a *meal together* that symbolizes what it actually does— nourish family members physically and spiritually. At a family meal, the parents mediate the growth of the children, making it the table at which life, in its small details and its great adventures, is shared by all. That meal, of course, has always been the setting within the family for the celebration of Passover, the setting for the Hebrew Seder just as it is for the Christian

Eucharist. Neither religious remembrance can be understood except through the mediation of family experience.

In the family of the Church, this mediation is evident in the relationship of the pope as the servant of the servants of God to and through the bishops and priests who are shepherds and pastors to the people, who are the flock. God is revealed through the medium of his creation, through the Church whose foundations were established by Jesus, through the Gospels and through the Church's teachers and what they teach. The sacraments are not mere set decorations or lodge insignia but are living spiritual symbols that contain and communicate the Christian Mystery of salvation, mediating it with no pale symbols at every significant stage of the human passage—cleansing waters and the taste of salt for the newborn, crusty bread and rich red wine to strengthen the growing, oil from growing things to seal the newly mature, a gentler oil to sign the hands of new priests and healing oil to comfort the sick. And, as in every family, with words that do not give life if they are stifled or left unspoken, words that must be spoken aloud in the admission of fault and the confession of sin and in responding with forgiveness, words to express their love and to bear the gravity of their vows as man and woman confer the sacrament of matrimony on each other.

There is no way to be a Catholic alone, no matter how exactly a spiritual recluse may honor the commandments. As we live in and through the relationships of our families and the multiple communities of our citizenship, callings and neighbor-hoods, we cannot be individualistic Christians. We understand best what we do when we become Catholics by realizing that we are not just joining a venerable institution, or an exclusive club, but simply becoming full members of a very big, and sometimes very boisterous, family.

A FAMILY OF CHURCHES

The late comedian Lenny Bruce once famously remarked that only to Catholicism does the culture award without protest the distinguishing definite article *The* as in *The Catholic Church*. While we may smile at his irony, *the* Catholic Church started out as a geographical grouping of *Churches*, that is, of Christian communities sown across the lands of the Mediterranean. A Christian community existed at Ephesus, for example, and a famous and sometimes fractious one at Corinth. These early communities had a relationship with each other and, as an illus-tration of their strong early ties with Judaism, with the mother Church at Jerusalem, for which, even as Catholics do for the Church at Rome today, they took up an annual collection. Paul addressed his letters to the Church *at* Corinth, the Church *at* Ephesus, and to other communities to whom he preached the Gospel. But the relationship of these local Churches is also made clear by Paul who unites them under the title, paid true if satiric tribute to twenty centuries later by Mr. Bruce, of *the* Church.[10]

SHARED FAITH AND PRACTICES

Despite their differences of location, history and even of specific problems, these local Churches shared the essentials of belief and practice, so that, taken together, they were understood then, as they are now, as *the* Church. Paul writes in strong and direct language to the Church at Corinth to correct the problems, some of them sexual, that he found among its people. He is disturbed at the confusion in worship sown by those practicing charismatic prayer and he chides the well-off for the disorders for which they seem responsible at the Eucharist. His letters make lively reading today as we catch his passion for the Gospel of Jesus Christ, his affection for the members of the community, and his recognition of the all-too-human problems, so like a big family's, with which he must deal to maintain the orthodoxy, unity and inner discipline of this Church.

If, two millennia later, we can recognize these believers as members of a family whose flaws may be seen first in them but also in ourselves, we also observe how much they held in common with the other local Churches. These include faith in Jesus as their Messiah and Lord; the sacramental life in the practice of baptism and the celebration of the Eucharist; ongoing instruction and learning through apostolic preaching; an expectation of the coming reign of God and, as in big families, the richest of all signs in their love for one another. Aside from these essentials, as the great Apostle insists, they are to enjoy freedom in all other matters, that is, a happy freedom from supervision in the rest of their lives.

These early Churches sensed their position in time as "between the coming, or reign, of God in Jesus Christ and its full realization at the end of history."[11] These people lived in what they understood as the *entre acte*, or in-between-times, with a sense of mission no different from that of the Catholic Church today, "to proclaim, celebrate, signify, and serve the coming reign of God."[12] We find terms in this period of the Catholic family's growth through these branches, the concepts that remain central to the Catholic Church today, the *kerygma*, or preaching "the message"; the *leitourgia*, the "liturgy" or "public work"; *marturia* or "witness"; and *diakonia* or ministry of "service."

The sense of the Church has deepened through the mining of meaning out of its origins by theologians, a process that is described by John Henry Cardinal Newman as the "development of doctrine." By this he did not mean the *invention* of new truths but a deepening theological understanding of the original message, revelation and experience of the Church as a family. In some ways this corresponds to the human family's gradual understanding of its beginning and its broadening through the experiments and reflection of science. Science does not add anything to the family inheritance but it identifies its contents as, for example, in the remarkable study of the human genome that reveals our long close relationship with each other, traced like the patterns of great rugs carpeting a long corridor, with its brokenness and blind alleys, of unrolling and sometimes unraveling history.

By the time of Vatican II (1962–1965) the Church, through its teaching authority, had established a far richer sense of the

Church that, as a family, is also, as we shall see, a Mystery and a sacrament.

A CHURCH OF CHURCHES, A FAMILY OF CHURCHES

The Catholic Church also remains a family of local Churches whose own identity does not disappear but is rather ratified and its *catholicity* affirmed in these various branches that, together, constitute the Church universal. We have always had the Church universal and the local Churches. Even in the non-capitalized letters of non-religious language, *catholic* means "universal" and, although people are most familiar with the *Roman* Catholic Church, it is not the only Church and we may speak of a Catholic Communion of Churches as those Churches, Roman and Eastern Rite alike, that are in full communion with the Bishop of Rome.

These Churches have their own rites but they cannot be understood merely as "rites" or "sects." The latter concept is not compatible with the ever-inclusive, familial nature of Catholicism. Sect comes from the Latin for a "faction" and refers to a group that separates from a larger religious body, professes moral rigor and an exclusivity that it enforces with strict social and religious discipline. Its members often see themselves as a pure group of Christians living in a hostile world, from which they flee, as they see it, to practice and to protect their beliefs.[13]

The larger family of Churches in union with Rome include the Armenian, Byzantine, Coptic, Ethiopian, East Syrian or Chaldean, West Syrian and Maronite. "Each of these," as

McBrien puts it, "is a Catholic church in communion with the Bishop of Rome; none of these is a *Roman* Catholic church. Catholicism...is neither narrowly Roman nor narrowly Western. It is universal in the fullest sense of the word.[14]

I'LL NEVER SPEAK TO HIM AGAIN...

A big family, indeed, and one not spared the kinds of splits and separations that are often found in large family groupings. The Eastern Orthodox Churches have been separate from Rome since the great East-West schism some seven hundred years ago. It is a slow process for sundered families to get together again or even to get back on speaking terms but this, at least, has taken place, especially under the inspiration of Pope John XXIII and the overtures made for dialogue about their relationship to the papacy by Pope John Paul II.

This quest for identity and unity is mirrored in the profound interest of ordinary people who journey, through searching genealogical records, back to their own beginnings to locate and learn more about the first, or founding, father and mother of the broader family of families of which they are members. It is not uncommon for them to learn that, much as in Catholicism, there have been splits and estrangements, often at moments of high sensitivity, such as marriage, in which the question of religious faith is frequently involved. Ordinary people want to heal these wounds and get to know the extended family of cousins whose ancestors they share and whose blood runs in their own veins.

CHAPTER THREE

Joining the Family

It is one thing to know something about a family and another thing to belong to one. Some families are overwhelming, as the Massachusetts Kennedys were said to be when Jacqueline Bouvier took that name through her marriage to John F. Kennedy in 1953. She did not, however, lose her own identity or traditions when she joined this clan but remained herself, never aloof but never so immersed that she allowed herself or her children to disappear within the touch football scrimmages of life that symbolized that boisterous and ambitious family. She became a Kennedy but never stopped being herself.

That is what it is like to become a member of the big family of the Catholic Church. You do not become a Catholic on the condition that you surrender your own personality at the Church door.

There are not only families but religious sects that consume rather than serve their members. Some other families regard those who enter them by marriage as taking on the markings, the moods and the manifest of their name and history, *That's why you married, isn't it, to become one of us?* Well, many people, including Jacqueline Bouvier, and maybe you, too, have to battle to maintain their own sense of themselves against the friendly fire of new in-laws who do not shoot but certainly take, at least under a kind of house arrest, those who cross, by whatever means, onto what they consider their turf, *You're one of us now....*

When men and women join the big family of the Church, they enter a very large and active family life but they are never asked, or expected, to place their own identities into the collection basket. Converts do not feel that they lose anything of themselves but rather that they recover the fullness of themselves. They do not stand holding their hats in the foyer but enter the home, much as they did that of a welcoming neighbor in childhood— you remember, all the kids hung out there—to find a place waiting for them in the midst of fully engaged family life.

WHAT DOES A FAMILY DO?

Families live in the present but exist for the future. Great families are of their nature *generative*, that is, concerned with and committed to giving and enriching life beyond themselves. Passivity is the greatest temptation for successful families but it is as fatal for them as *hemophilia* was for the Romanovs. The family may be understood as a model of the Catholic Church because its dynamics, and the events associated with them, are essentially the same.

A family, we may say, gives and nourishes life and its many symbols and well-remembered traditions are in the service of that new life. The family is constituted by a set of human relationships—husband and wife, father and mother and children—whose creativity depends on, and is expressed through, intimacy: that sacred and safe closeness in which people pass beyond surface appearances and attractions to reveal and to discover the truth about themselves and each other, to grow not in response to an intellectual lesson or a formal command but out of the unguarded human sharing that is, at the same time, the family's greatest strength and foremost vulnerability. Only in intimacy do human persons become fully alive and fully themselves and, only because of intimacy, are they thereby subjected to the Mystery of hurt and loss.

AUTHORITY IN A FAMILY, AUTHORITY IN THE CHURCH

Americans, and many other peoples in the world, have trouble with authority because they do not understand its true meaning and its centrality as a dynamic of generativity in life. When most people speak of, or shrink back from, authority, as in the bumper sticker *Resist Authority*, they are reacting not to genuine authority but to a concept that, despite its similar root, is a world away in meaning. That is *authoritarianism*, an exercise of power over others in order to control them. We speak of

dictatorships as authoritarian regimes, that is, forms of govern-
ment in which power is exercised over the many below by the
one—or small group—at the top.

Authority, on the other hand, comes from the Latin *augere*,
and means to create, to increase, to make able to grow. Healthy
authority, the kind that helps people to become fully themselves, is not a function of titles, abstract analysis, birthright, the
smooth use of public relations or the manipulation of power.
Healthy authority is always and ever rooted in healthy human
relationships.

ALWAYS THERE

Such authority is the unseen but very real dynamic in every
life-giving and spirit-enlarging human relationship. Ordinary
people tell us very accurately about the impact of the significant
others, as they are called, in their lives. They want to tell us
about these relationships because they feel enlarged and free as
a result of experiencing them with good parents, teachers, super-
visors, pastors and other similar figures. Or they can feel dimin-
ished and less free, bound by the controlling effects of those
who, responding to their own ill-understood needs, exercise
power to restrict, direct and make them conform rather then
give them the space and vote of confidence they need to mature
from within themselves.

We observe this kind of development only in human relationships in which one person relates to another in order to help
the latter grow into his or her fullness. Parents *author* their chil-

dren in this fashion and exercise authority not through rules but through the thousand ways they relate to them to initiate and guide their growth to maturity and to the mastery of their talents. In family or Church, *healthy authority* frees rather than dominates. It employs discipline, limits and challenges not to inhibit but to facilitate the growth of others. Teachers exercise such authority in relationship to their students, pastors to their flocks, and creators to their works. If Christ is described as speaking "as one having authority," he clarifies this by saying that he has come that others might have "life and life to the full." As fresh air opens our lungs authority expands our spirits. Astringent authoritarianism, on the other hand, causes us to curl and contract, closing us off to both fresh air and Spirit.

CHURCH AUTHORITY

The world feels two ways about power. Obsessed by it, people are drawn to it and repelled by it at the same time. While the Catholic Church has been both envied and reviled for its supposed mastery of power, it is actually authority that makes it work as a Church. Thinking about becoming a Catholic, persons might be attracted by the power that Catholicism is said to possess. The great English writer G. K. Chesterton once said that he became a Catholic to have his sins forgiven. He respected what is known as *the power of the keys*, generally understood to mean Christ's endowing Peter and the other apostles, in his name, to forgive sins or to withhold forgiveness. While this sacramental delegation is spoken of as a power it is, in fact, an authorization that changes this action from an impersonal verdict to a highly personal judgment in which it is not the apostles' power to control heavenly destiny but their capacity to author spiritual growth that is crucial to its meaning and its efficacy.

In this example of a *sacramental* transaction—the most distinguishing mark of Catholic life—we understand better how and why authority is exercised within this Church. The sacramental life of the Church is a dynamic environment that depends on and is expressed, at every stage, by the Church as a People of God making its pilgrimage through time as the Jewish people made theirs through the dusty exile of Egypt. This is a family on the move, as we see in the Gospels, its members falling in love, marrying and being given in marriage, giving and nurturing life, worshiping God and seeking his Kingdom, breaking their idols to reestablish the covenant, supporting each other in every trial and comforting each other in sickness and death, a great moveable feast of a Church in which nothing spiritual takes place that is not *mediated* through human relationships and is never achieved outside our relationships with each other.

Such a Church is not protoplasmic, nor could it ever be found inside an individual's head or heart—no matter how noble—or in someone who despises the world or other people. Catholicism, as a Church *authoring* spiritual growth, centers itself *on the human*; the authority it claims for its pope, bishops, and pastors is rooted in their commitment to the life-giving and life-enlarging relationships that they form and support with all the spiritual resources of the Church. Catholics may think that they suffer or pray alone but that is impossible in the big family of the Church where its consciousness of being a community—a Mystery of people in decisive and defining relationship to each other—is foremost in its understanding of itself.

FAMILY REUNION

A similar project has been underway, now advancing, now pausing to catch its breath, in the Catholic family under the title of the Ecumenism, from the Greek *oikodome*, "the household of God." Thomas Stransky defines it as "a process that is directed toward the achievement of unity among all Christian Churches, and ultimately among all religious communities."[15] Even as in the current passion for genealogies, the central question concerns the *author* of the family and the claims through that title to the possession of *authority*, so in ecumenical studies the father figure, the pope, and the way various Christian churches relate to him, stand at the center of concern. This is a new version of the search for the father that is the theme of such myths as that of Telemachus and that lies beneath so much contemporary longing for our deepest human roots.

Anybody interested in Catholicism soon learns the very same thing that a person does about a human family they are entering by marriage or adoption: estrangements and long cease-fires of no open hostility—but no conversation either—are found in every extended family. Some do not even respond to the invitation to a family reunion. As in the ecumenical movement, reconciliation is a slow process that demands great patience and understanding, that may suffer setbacks or a loss of interest at times, and yet, as long as openness and good will exist, continues towards its goal.

In the history of the Church, much as in the stories of big families, such estrangements and splits arise over misunderstandings and misinterpretations of words, agreements, promises and intentions. Splits have occurred in the history of the Catholic Church over single words, or single words boiled down to syllables, and held, soaked in the hundred-proof venom of grudges, like Molotov cocktails to be lighted and lobbed across the lines, dividing the family into factions that curse each other as heretics.

We pause, like museum-goers who remove the earphones, cutting off the disembodied voice that is telling them what they are looking at and how they should respond, so that we may open our whole selves to the Church whose image spills like light out of its frame. Let it flood through us, this Church communicating from its depths to our depths about the kind of family it is.

CHAPTER FOUR

Feeding the Family
Mystery and Sacrament / Church and Jesus

We stand quietly now, the spinning tape of interpretations stilled, the "doors of perception" cleansed, as the mystical poet Blake urged, so that we may "see the world as it is, infinite." That captures the Catholic sacramental viewpoint exactly. For Catholics the universe, measured in spaces so great as the cosmos itself or so small as the individual heart, offers a revelation of the Mystery of God for it is, in a sense, a paper lantern lit by the divine.

Religious mysteries, especially this central one, are not to be solved. They are rather to be plumbed as the depths of the ocean are to be searched without exhausting or fully comprehending them. But for Catholics, the revelation glows in the universe itself that, as Pope Paul VI expressed it, is "imbued with the divine." Through this sacramental sense, Catholicism constantly attunes itself to the signals of life given off by all creation, seeing into and symbolizing them in ways that match and enhance us as human persons.

We may better understand the sacramental life of Catholicism if we continue to stand, our headset and distractions discarded, in front of this masterpiece of creation that now speaks in its own way to our complete personalities. Art that addresses only the intellect waters down its own blood as it turns into pale and abstract geometry that is disengaged from our persons and our place of life. Art that stirs only the emotions sells itself out, and us short, as sentimentality or propaganda. True art converses symbolically with every layer of our being and consciousness. Sacramental Catholicism speaks in our many human languages to the yearnings beneath them, conversing not with a part but with the whole human personality. The fundamental presupposition of sacramental Catholicism is that our own Mystery reflects the great Mystery, that the unity of personality reflects the unity of the universe and the Mystery of the unity of the Godhead, that Mystery of the relationships of Divine Persons with each other, a shimmer of whose awe we catch in our relationships with each other.

SACRAMENTA PROPTER HOMINES

One of the oldest and most trustworthy of Catholic sayings is *Sacramenta propter homines*: the sacraments are for human persons. They are not gifts to the angels, entitlements for the blessed or advertisements for the Divine. They are addressed to men and women, in care of the human condition, to assist, encourage, feed, comfort and console us as we journey through lives that are mistakenly called ordinary. The sacraments provide grace, the very life of God, more like the air we breathe than a food supplement, a mystical tattoo or a spiritual souvenir. The sacraments are, therefore, understandable only if we understand human personality. We cannot really grasp anything about them if we have a corrupted or inaccurate notion of the human person. One of the most damaging distortions of the person is found in the divided model that is a corruption of the traditional Catholic appreciation of the wholeness of personality. Such a division makes sacrilege of the sacramental by splitting the person into warring elements of body and soul, intellect and emotion, spirit and flesh, setting people against themselves, making them feel guilty, for example, for being human and experiencing healthy sexual feelings.

These tyrannizing distortions interfere with our understanding ourselves, our world, each other and the Mystery in which our lives are led. Distortions of the human damage our sacramental sense, pulling us back from what we should embrace in the Mystery of ourselves-as-we-are and of the sacramental life-as-it-is, geared, at one and the same moment, to the overlapping and interpenetrating mysteries of our glorious imperfection and of our extraordinary existence. *Sacramenta propter homines*: The sacraments are for people just like us.

Human beings are sensual, sexual and spiritual all at the same time. So, too, are the sacraments. They do not estrange us from but make us comfortable with ourselves and with God's constant self-disclosure through creation. So we say, "*I* am baptized" rather than, "My *soul* is baptized," and, "*I* receive the Eucharist" rather than, "My *soul* receives the Eucharist."

THE CHURCH AS SACRAMENT

But what does a term such as *Mystery* mean in the context of the sacraments? How is the Church, as Catholics believe, a sacrament that exists before any of the seven individual sacraments that we will presently examine? To understand the Church as sacrament, we must first understand Jesus as the first, or, as scholars express it, the *primordial* sacrament. These notions only sound complicated and defining these terms helps us to grasp their full meaning.

Mystery is a term that refers "to the infinite incomprehensibility of God."[16] In the New Testament, *Mystery—mysterion* (Greek) and *mysterium* (Latin)—refers to God's saving plan for us, his providential will for all of our human history. The Easter Vigil ceremonies are called mysteries because they are rites that incorporate the believing community (the Church) into salvation history, associating this believing community with God's plan that is revealed only slowly in the calendar of time that measures our earthly lives.

The Church teaches that in its principal liturgical rites, the sacraments, Catholics "experience the love and power of God (grace) that flows from Christ's Passion, death, and Resurrection."[17] Before the list of these official sacraments was made final in the twelfth century, the term *sacrament* bore even richer connotations. As Francis observes, "Used originally to name any manifestation of God's power and love in space and time, sacrament...also conveys a sense of hiddenness.... (t)he hidden plan of God manifested in human history and made accessible to those who have faith."[18]

ONE MYSTERY, TWO FACES

The great German theologian Karl Rahner holds that "...there is only one fundamental mystery that has two aspects: the mystery that is the being of God and the mystery that is the saving presence of the incomprehensible God in human history." Rahner goes on to say that all of our "knowledge exists only in reference to this unfathomable mystery of God's life with us, a mystery that is expressed by three mutually implicated doctrines of the faith: the Trinity, the Incarnation, and the doctrine of grace."[19]

Catholics believe that they are caught up in religious Mystery, the Mystery of living with God, linked to the eternal through the portals of the sacraments that express and allow us to experience this eternal Mystery in the lesser Mystery of unfolding time. There is no place untouched by or cut off from this fundamental Mystery of our life in God. The terms *Mystery* and *sacrament* have always been associated with each other in the history of the Catholic Church. We cannot, then, understand the sacraments outside of the Church that, as expressed in Vatican II, is "itself a sacrament and even a basic sacrament."[20] The Catholic Church understands itself, rather than Baptism, as the *first* sacrament.

JESUS AS FIRST SACRAMENT

Deeper than this, however, the Church recognizes the priority of Jesus as the original or "primordial" sacrament. What does this mean? Primordial is defined: "Beginning or happening first in a sequence of time...radical, fundamental...basic principle."[21] Perhaps more tellingly for us, the very word *primordial* comes from *primus*, meaning "first," and *ordiri*, meaning "to begin a web." The anchor, the root, the strand from which the web will be woven—these give us some sense, in the language of our progression in time, of how everything in the Church flows first from Jesus Christ, and how, then, from the Church the sacraments themselves flow. They would be orphans and empty if they did not come from Jesus as the first sacrament, the authoring sacrament, the original sign and symbol of the *mysterion*, and then from the Church as steward of the Mystery and the author of the sacraments for us.

The sacraments are not incidentals of history, like Plymouth Rock or the Pantheon, but signs of God's presence and action in history itself; they are not the insignia, passwords or secret handshakes and ceremonies of progressively graded membership in a thousand fraternal organizations. They are not a dues-free life membership in an exclusive club but a way of life, the dynamic symbols of God's effulgence in our human condition and of our utterly free access to God through the intervention in history of Jesus Christ. Jesus in his humanity is the first sacrament and his Church the next in this web of divine energy tapped by the individual sacraments that are fitted so perfectly to our human lives. Our best insight into them as living and transforming experiences derives from the very human family life to whose most sacred moments they are linked and whose significance they underscore and enlarge.

CHURCH FAMILY AND SACRAMENTS

We are brought into life in a family, depending on the love of parents and, indeed, our physical as well as spiritual contact with them, if we are to survive and to flourish. We are washed at birth and cared for throughout infancy, given a seat at the table at which we learn and grow in our relationships with our parents and other family members. Life is celebrated and mediated at this table and, as we have noted, at the family meals eaten there. The Eucharist, the body and blood of the Lord, is not manna or a wished-for wonder but the true presence of Jesus Christ through which we are nourished for the life, death and resurrection cycle found every day in every life.

We are confirmed in our personal identity by the Church as we are by the family. We are sealed in the Mystery by the ongoing sacramental prayer event—as linked as the Trinity—of baptism, confirmation and Eucharist. By these we are nourished and strengthened to accept fully the calling we first received at birth, so that we may bring our own gifts into life, placing ourselves at risk as we carry on the family tradition and pursue the human imperative to author new life and new families. The family is the context for the sacrament of marriage that symbolizes God's covenant with his people and Jesus' covenant with the Church and is conferred by man and woman on each other as they become husband and wife. So, too, the Church responds with the sacrament of orders to acknowledge and seal those called to serve as ministers of the sacraments and pastors of the flock.

The sacramental system is gauged to that constant of the human condition that is so linked to our gains and losses—our human vulnerability to time and chance. Nothing symbolizes this awareness better than the Sacrament of Reconciliation, popularly known as "confession," and the Anointing of the Sick, once known, in a way that beggars the better understanding that we have of it now, as the Last Rites. In the Sacrament of Reconciliation, Catholics acknowledge their sinfulness, forgive themselves as they seek forgiveness, express their contrition and amendment of life, and are sealed by the words of absolution from Jesus through their priest. The priest's identity is specified through the sacrament of orders, through which he is authorized to celebrate the sacrament of the Eucharist—the Paschal Mystery of incarnation, death and resurrection in which we are immersed in our daily lives.

Nothing matches our human condition better than this sacrament which makes room for, rather than exiles, the sinning class of which we are all paid-up members. At Vatican II, the late Albert Cardinal Meyer of Chicago intervened in the bishops' discussion of the nature of the Church to remind them then, and us now, that the Church may be best understood as "the home of sinners." So, too, the Anointing of the Sick, once thought to be only for those on their deathbeds, is better appreciated as a Mystery that heals and strengthens us as we face any illness, in each of which lie curled traces of the Mystery of loss, separation and death over which Jesus triumphed in his Resurrection.

Jesus is the first sacrament, the author of the sacraments, and the Church is sacrament, too, derived from Jesus to reflect the Mystery of the world to itself and to celebrate the sacraments that are a perfect fit for our humanity.

CHAPTER FIVE

What the Family Believes

Tolstoy sighs at all that he has seen of human wonder and sorrow as he touches his pen to paper and writes one of his most famous sentences, "Happy families are all alike; every unhappy family is unhappy in its own way."[22]

But even if we have looked on less of our condition than the great Russian novelist, we know that even happy families must meet their daily quota of unexpected challenges; sorrows are delivered to all doors at daybreak along with the milk and long before the mail. Indeed, a happy family actively accepts, rather than passively suffers, the pattern and rhythm of the Paschal Mystery that stands at the very center of Catholicism both as a Church, as a faith or, more essentially, as a way of life that fits the glories and dangers of being human. Healthy families are not abstractions but incarnations, flesh and blood realities of men and women who give and receive life through their relationships with each other.

Whether our relationships give life or not depends on our readiness to undergo the deaths, large and small and almost beyond counting, that come in different ways every day. Among these claims, as stubborn as dug-in troops, we may easily recognize our urges to protect and control our own sovereignty by keeping others at a safe distance. These must be given up willingly if we are to make room for others in our lives and to give them the freedom of movement that both nourishes and reveals true love. A family begins only because lovers accept these deaths to their self-containment, the selfishness whose signature notes are heard first in the overture and then throughout every movement of the symphonic Mystery of our existence.

THE FAMILY AND THE PASCHAL MYSTERY

The loving family—the happy family—lives joyfully, but never without sorrows. Indeed, they are ever with the sorrows that are so thoroughly sown as to seem inlaid and inseparable from the simple surrenders of self that are the lifeblood of all love and of any spiritual and sacramental sense of life. The happy family accepts these deaths that open it to that full measure of life that thrives even within the restraints of time and the ever-present hazards of chance. This readiness to yield itself up enables such a family to glimpse the eternal lightning that flashes its greater Mystery within the lesser Mystery of time's unreeling hours and minutes.

Lovers not only lay down their lives so that a family may have life but the family itself, this Mystery in miniature, also lays down its life to free its members to bring newer families into existence. Every happy family is born, dies and rises again, every happy family lives out the Paschal Mystery that is at the heart of the belief and being of the Catholic Church.

This is what the family of Catholicism believes and everything else it believes and practices flows from this Mystery. What it believes and practices about the cycle of dying and rising are as interwoven in the life of a happy family as the harvested selfishness of broken hearts and bad times are in the families that are unhappy, each in their own way.

What does the big family of the Church believe in? What would be the signs of faith on the earth when the Son of Man comes? These questions may be answered in a formal theological manner, as they are in the *Catechism of the Catholic Church,* but even these answers depend on how Catholics themselves live. Simple adages, like sayings jotted in the margins of the family Bible, have supported this insight throughout the centuries. Look into this family whose life is immersed in Mystery and see how it prays, see how its inner life flowers in its daily life, see what it believes in the teachings that it lives out in such profound and yet quotidian Mystery. The Church praying is the Church believing.

THE CHURCH AT PRAYER

We return to the fundamental understanding of the sacraments as the Church at prayer, reading in these symbols that sing of life, death and resurrection the reality of Jesus as the first sacrament, the origin of all life for the Church as sacrament and, within this Mystery, the sacraments that initiate, sustain and symbolize everything the Church believes and teaches.

Signs

The sacraments, according to Saint Thomas Aquinas, are first of all signs that instruct and make us mindful of the reality that they signify. As Catholics participate in the sacramental rituals, they profess their faith in that which, even unseen, is spiritually real to them. The family of Catholicism believes that these signs are not mere directional guides but that they are *authoritative* in the sense that they author, or proclaim, faith.

Worship

Secondly, these signs express worship. Through them, as Richard McBrien observes, "we participate ritually, i.e., through signs, in Christ's own worship of the Father." His summary catches the majesty of the sacramental experience: "The Lord's Supper, or Eucharist, is linked from the beginning with the Passover meal, at which Israel gratefully (eucharistically) relived its deliverance from the bondage of Egypt and prayed for the coming of the Messiah. The early Church spoke of Christ as its Passover who had been sacrificed (1 Corinthians 5:7) and related its own fellowship meals to Christ's sacrificial action (1 Corinthians 10:16–17)."[23]

Unity

The sacraments also signify the unity of the Church because the belief expressed in each sacrament manifests what the Church believes. It is the "faith *of* the Church," as McBrien says, and "the faith mediated to the individual *by* the Church."[24] The sacraments signify and proclaim the faith held in common by the Church and by its members.

Presence

The sacraments are also signs that Christ is present, that God is active in the family life of the Church. In other words, since Christ is both God and man, his human actions, alive in the sacraments that remember and celebrate them, transcend the time that limits us. The sacraments are not *tableaux vivant* but experiences in which God, who is outside time, is present, through Jesus, in the here and now, as much in living relationship to us as we are to each other in a family. This transaction between God and us, Jesus alive to us, is signified in every sacrament. They are, therefore, dynamic sources of our understanding what the Catholic family, or Church, believes.

THE FAMILY ALBUM

Inspect the family album or the videos of any happy family and find that the pictures organize themselves around its least adorned and least self-conscious moments of intense relationship, in the way, imperfect, to be sure, in which its members love each other. That is why, as people leaf through such collections of symbolic family moments, they smile, gently and spontaneously and in their faces we can read the family history and actually feel the strength of the relationships that link its members together even long after they have been dispersed to establish new families on the same foundations of faithful and loving relationships. Researchers tell us that, as people reach the end of their lives, they recall the simple family gatherings and trips, rather than expensive vacations or luxurious possessions, as the best times of their lives. This is what is celebrated in the family album's pictures, sacramental in themselves, of the sacramental passages of the family—of baptisms, confirmations, first Eucharist and, of course, marriages—the sacred moments as, in an endless cycle, the head river family divides to send its energy streaming in new directions.

BAPTISM

We are sometimes puzzled that Jesus himself should have been baptized by John. Theologians, as we have noted, speak of Jesus as the primordial sacrament, that is, the originating sacrament. What, then, is the significance of that moment in the Jordan river when God speaks of Jesus as "beloved son"? This event is the unique creative sacramental moment that invests the Church and the individual sacraments with their grace and power, that makes them live and transmit God's life to us. This baptism of Jesus by John is understood by Catholics as the *first* sacred moment that engenders the preeminent and predominant Mystery of God's entering history in Jesus.

Catholics do not believe that this was just a critical moment in the life of a great person, such as Alexander's first sense of a calling to conquer the world or Saul of Tarsus's vision on the road to Damascus. It is rather the transforming event in what we call salvation history.

As scholar Kenan Osborne expresses it, the baptism of Jesus in the Jordan "was deeper than any immersion in water, it is the immersion of Jesus into God's own self.... He truly is *the* baptized."[25] This is a total and complete giving in which Jesus "keeps nothing of himself back," a revelatory episode about the Mystery of God's inner life in relationship to our inner lives. That Jesus "is baptized with his entire human being...tells us something about the very locus in which Jesus' humanness began to be...something about the beginning of his very incarnate life." We might well rub our eyes in wonder at this communication of God's spirit, that, as Osborne instructs us, "is what primordially the baptism of Jesus is all about: the communication of the Spirit of God so that *Jesus begins to be*...this baptized humanness of Jesus is what baptism is all about."[26]

BEYOND RITUAL

Our view of baptism is compromised if we examine it only as a ritual. Here we behold Jesus as *the baptized* and read the meaning of this dynamic sacrament in Jesus' "human nature and its relationship to the Godhead." Baptism is to be understood as a "prayer event" in which the community celebrates a fundamental belief, "the *relationship* between God (as also Christ) and a given human person, since God's gift is not some thing but his very self, and the giving of self to another self and the mutual return of self to self is always a relationship."[27]

Baptism is indeed a *Mystery*, as the Church fathers called it, and we understand better why it is the great sacramental culmination, along with confirmation and Eucharist, of entrance into the Church, for those becoming Catholic and joining the Church's big family.

But it is a *Mystery* that we humans can grasp because it manifests itself in a *relationship* between persons, a *Mystery* uttered and experienced in the concepts of friendship and love, in the experience of fulfilling and fulfilled intimacy in which we are revealed and reveal ourselves to each other. A powerful transaction occurs in our lives when someone else reveals himself or herself to us because, by the light of their revelation, we find ourselves more fully revealed, for we are now able to see what we were blind to in ourselves until we entered this relationship with somebody else.

That is the transaction—the something that goes on between us and others in every look, thought and gesture of friendship and love—that allows us to understand how God reveals and communicates himself to us and how, by the light of that grace, we are revealed to ourselves as well. We already know something about this precisely because we are human. Catholics believe that this transmittal of God's life to us follows on, flows from, and symbolizes sacramentally, God's giving of his spirit so that Jesus begins to be, that a *relationship*—a concept that we can grasp if never exhaust—exists between God and the individual person baptized.

THE MYSTERY/THE MYSTERY

We are not members of a faceless mass, whose lives and deeds are forgotten, if they were ever noted, by a God who passes on, as history does, to other things. We are not forgotten nobodies or unknown soldiers, as we speak of the lost whose identity we preserve by a relationship of memory and regret. We are, through baptism, complete individuals, whole persons with whom God establishes a knowing and loving relationship. We are baptized into a Mystery that is the Mystery of Catholicism. God's nature is expressed in terms that are second nature to us, those of relationship, and that is why we are sealed by the Trinitarian relationship in the name of the Father, the Son and the Holy Spirit. This relationship is real and our best insight into it comes from our experience of loving relationships with each other.

The Church's teaching that baptism is necessary is not, therefore, dictated by some imperative of membership rules but by the nature of the relationship that God establishes with us in and through this event that is the Church at prayer. The Church has always taught the necessity of baptism, based on Jesus' commandment to do so (Matthew 28:19–20). The family estrangement that occurred in Christianity at the Reformation does not mean that other Christian denominations do not baptize validly. Indeed, the Church recognizes that this is so and never rebaptizes someone who has already been validly baptized. We receive this sacrament only once because the Church believes that, as is also true of Confirmation and Holy Orders, it confers a *character* on us when we receive it, the seal of God's taking us into relationship to himself. Adults who wish to become Catholics are prepared for the Holy Saturday night *Rite of Christian Initiation of Adults*, the *R.C.I.A.*, as it is termed. They join the big family of the Church as it celebrates the Paschal Mystery of the Life, Death and Resurrection of Jesus that is the fundamental religious Mystery that identifies and allows us to identify its rhythms in our own lives.

CONFIRMATION

Baptism, Eucharist and confirmation were once intimately linked in the celebration of the Paschal Mystery and recent liturgical renewal enables us to see their integral relationship as the Church at prayer and the Church revealing the theologically seamless connection of these sacraments in its proclamation of this bedrock Mystery. As Jesus is the originating sacrament, it follows that his Church is sacrament as it signs and symbolizes the action of God in our lives through this trinity of Mystery of initiating, anointing and nourishing those who thereby enter a new relationship with God. Through the anointing with chrism and the touch of the hand of the minister, the inflowing of the Spirit is confirmed in the context of the initiation rites. It is understandable that many theologians have held that baptism and confirmation are not easily separated and that their historical division into different ceremonies blurred the ancient sense of their symbolic integrity.

It surprises even many lifelong Catholics when they learn that, until a century ago, the family of the Church considered baptism and confirmation as aspects of one sacrament and administered the latter before the Eucharist and before reconciliation (what many still call "confession"). The separation of these sacraments that are best understood as integral to the rite of initiation gave confirmation a distinctive moment in ceremonies usually conducted by the local bishop and that were popularly interpreted as a strengthening step on the way to being an adult Christian and to bearing witness bravely in the world. The slight slap of the bishop's hand, no longer part of the ceremony, was thought to symbolize this transition to adult responsibilities. This formulation, although recalled with affection, not to say nostalgia, by many older Catholics, isolated confirmation as less a vital aspect of the initiation rite and more as the kind of rite of passage associated with puberty or the educational equivalent of moving from primary to secondary school.

The liturgical renewal of Vatican Council II reconnected confirmation with baptism and the Eucharist as intimately related and integral to the initiation rites and, in the 1972 publication of the R.C.I.A., this Mystery, as it has been called, this Paschal Mystery that is the pattern of the new relationship with God that converts enter when they become full members of the family of Catholicism, is restored to the context of these climactic rites. The relational core of entering this family, and its link to baptism, is underscored by the desirability of having the same godparents for confirmation as those who served this function for the individual's baptism. Both baptism and confirmation awaken in those who receive them the missionary dynamic, the going-out-of-itself, the readiness to suffer disintegration, in order to author life for others, or achieve a higher level of reintegration, a process that creative people experience every day, that is the creative and generative fundamental of family life and of life in the family of the Church.

THE EUCHARIST

The Eucharist symbolizes and, indeed, realizes what the Church believes as God's presence in history, in the concrete times, places and relationships of our lives, in the fullest possible way. Eucharist, from the Greek word for *Thanksgiving*, is "the sacramental celebration of the Paschal Mystery (i.e., Christ's dying and rising for humankind) in a context of praise and thanks for all that God has done and continues to do.... [T]he Holy Spirit is called down on the assembly that it might become the Body of Christ, the People of God."[28]

In the celebration of the Eucharist, we find the rich and real Catholic family spiritual inheritance, and we discover in this sacrament, symbolically and truly, what Catholics believe about the presence and continuing and defining action of the Risen Christ in the Church, in the world, in the panorama of history and in our individual lives. This is the Church praying, celebrating and believing as it understands itself as the Body of

Christ and the People of God. Ask the family members why they go to Church and many will reply, with a subtle sense of how this Paschal Mystery speaks so powerfully and authoritatively to them, "For the Mass," or, in short, for the "one bread" of this sacrament that, as Paul wrote (1 Corinthians 10:17) makes them one body in Christ.

The Eucharist is thus intimately related to what theologians term the "water bath" of Baptism and the "oil anointing" of confirmation in the initiation rites of Holy Saturday in which those men and women becoming Catholics receive these sacraments and become full members of the family of the Catholic Church. This experience is not a dramatic fiction or a special effect but a profound experience of the reality of their relationship through the Risen Jesus with the Father and the Spirit. This is the *Good News*.

Both the Old and New Testaments are filled with meals, real and ritual, and our understanding of the Eucharist sees a relationship between the feast of the Eucharist and the Jewish Passover meal that always celebrated God's liberation of, and ongoing covenant with, the Jewish people. As Duffy observes, a meal celebration of this kind "offers a model for understanding Christ's liberation of the world from sin through his death."[29]

THE HISTORY OF THE EUCHARIST AND RELIGIOUS LANGUAGE

The history of the Eucharist has been filled with disputes and intellectual emphases that reflect, as one would expect, the impact of the larger forces (such as the barbarian invasions and destruction of Christian centers) on how the Eucharist was discussed at different times and what aspects of it arrested the attention of theologians and Church officials. While we cannot explore all of these, one of them does illustrate a transformation of religious language and symbol that is found throughout the history of all religions. That is the loss of the metaphorical sense of religious language, this many layered symbolic expression, sometimes described as mytho-poetic, contrasted with concrete language or the stop sign level of communication discussed earlier.

The hostile invasions of Christian lands and centers many centuries ago "devastated the religious, cultural, and sociopolitical world of Augustine and his contemporaries," resulting in "an impoverishment of religious and ethnic culture from which people drew their symbolic resources and inspiration."[30] Metaphor, the native tongue of religious Mystery cannot be understood literally, that is, in its *denotation*, but only in the richness of the aura of meanings that plays around it, that is, in its *connotations*. Metaphors do not provide concrete measurements. Instead, "(t)hey deliver," as Joseph Campbell puts it, "more than just an intellectual concept, for such is their inner character that they provide a sense of actual participation in a realization of transcendence."[31]

If religion is directed to the imagination and metaphor is its native tongue, religion is strongly and adversely affected by any loss of fluency in speaking or understanding this special language.

That has happened often in history with the result that the metaphor becomes concretized and the focus shifts away from its spiritual meaning to its severely limited stop-sign-like denotation. This distorts our ability to grasp or talk about anything but a concept's hardened shell while we let its true contents spill out, unnoticed and wasted. The metaphor *Promised Land*, for example, has suffered from being reduced to a literal concept. Stripped of its spiritual meaning as a region of the heart we can all enter, it becomes an embattled piece of geography, a religious Verdun over which men wage seemingly unending wars.

This shift to the concrete is illustrated in the Eucharist by the alteration of focus, in symbolically deprived times, away from the meal and onto the menu, the cookbook, and, at times, even to the chef. In the medieval period, in which the number of those receiving the Eucharist dropped drastically, sensational and fantastic stories abounded of the host and wine as miracle vehicles or as subjects of theological urban legends, such as the problem of what to do if a priest entered a bakery and consecrated all the bread in its ovens and display cases.

This transformation also led to viewing and valuing the Eucharist as talisman issuing into such bizarre practices as men and women hurrying from Church to Church to be present only at the elevation of the host and cup because of the belief, degraded by this concreteness, that looking at the Eucharist preserved youthfulness.[32] A vestige of this survived well into the twentieth century in which the practice of visiting the Eucharist in as many Churches as possible on Holy Thursday sponsored the calculation of graces gained in bank-account fashion.

The completion of such swift rounds of sacrament visitations made the Eucharist mysterious but destroyed its essential Mystery. This was also reflected later in an intense preoccupation with surface questions about the composition of the wine, the flour in the bread and a buzzing hive of obsessive concrete details that debased and distorted both sacramental understanding and practice. This generated long, involved and confusing discussions about how Christ was present in the Eucharist and to pastoral practice that distracted people from understanding the fundamental and inclusive meaning of the Eucharist at the center of their lives.

FROM THE FAMILY TO THE INDIVIDUAL

As the Eucharist encapsulates essential Catholic beliefs, so its history encapsulates the ebb and flow of spiritual styles and theological discussions. The most significant of these, for our purposes, was the movement away from seeing the Church as a community and our belonging to it through our relationships with the Risen Lord and each other, to an emphasis on the Eucharist in splendid isolation, as an instrument—part magic wand and part global positioning system—in the pursuit of individual piety and perfection. The Eucharist became the baton held aloft by the long distance runner in the competitive holiness syndrome in which the emphasis was placed on the isolated ascetics seeking to make their souls perfect as athletes do their bodies. Not for nothing is the long distance runner thought lonely, as he sprints away from the community in these Eucharistic Olympics that wrenched the Eucharist so far away from a community- and family-centered celebration of being one body in Christ.

The Eucharist came to be received only on special occasions and, although Masses were said, they were often offered in isolation, multiplied by priests standing at altars physically side by side but spiritually and liturgically worlds apart. In old country rectories at the middle of the twentieth century one could still find altars at which the priest offered daily Mass by himself; its celebration daily in Church, so familiar today as to seem an immemorial custom, was not common practice. A favorite mid-twentieth century spiritual book, My Mass, symbolized how the Eucharist was approached both by celebrant and congregation as a highly personal focus of their one-on-one relationship to Jesus. Only after Pope Pius X issued his decree on frequent communion in the first decade of that century did more frequent reception of the Eucharist and daily Mass become commonplace in the Catholic culture. An impulse to reform such practices waited until Vatican II and its restoration of the sense of the Eucharist as a communal celebration and, for example, of the practice of concelebration by several priests at one time. Historically, therefore, we witness in the attitudes toward the Eucharist the hazards common to all religions: the temptation to concretize and privatize them so that their sacramental sense and meaning is perverted if not destroyed.

THE FAMILY AND THE EUCHARIST

The Catholic community, the big family of the Church, came into existence after the Resurrection of Jesus, after, as we might say, the completion of that Paschal cycle of *Incarnation, Death* and *Resurrection* that we find in the life of Jesus and whose pattern we recognize in our own. The Resurrection of Jesus is the decisive event in everything we recognize about Jesus as First Sacrament infusing life into the Church as sacrament and the source of the sacraments that define its life and ministry. It is the Jesus who overcomes death who initiates everything we know about the origins of the family of the Church and its sacramental life. We can never reach this profound spiritual understanding if we focus only on the concrete denotations of details and circumstances that abound in the sweep of salvation history.

As Father Osborne underscores this matter, one "should clearly emphasize that the eucharist, both in its reality and in its theological interpretation, is a post-resurrection event and depends very much on the action of the Spirit of Jesus which was 'sent' as an integral part of the post-Easter event of 'instituting the Church.'"[33] The Eucharist, then, is the Christian community, or the Church as a family, celebrating "the real presence of the Lord in their communal meal...the eucharist as a meal, i.e., people-eating-together, is a sacrament or sign *of* the presence of the risen Lord *to* the community of believers."[34]

WHAT THE FAMILY BELIEVES ABOUT THE EUCHARIST

The Church teaches as it prays and the Church family believes as it prays and the center of this is the Eucharist in which Jesus is truly present—not some wisp, fantasy or invested longing—but Jesus himself, the Word made flesh, Jesus the person just as he is. This firm belief that all of Jesus, rather than one aspect of him, is present invokes the wholeness of his personality, his *humanness*, as scholars speak of it, in real relationship to us and to the community, or family, of the Church.

What is the basis for this notion of the Real Presence of Jesus in the Eucharist that feeds and unites the family that lives in real relationship with him? As Father Osborne puts it, drawing on the renewal of Vatican II, we must understand that the foundation of this Real Presence "is not the eucharist, but (a) the real presence of the Logos in the humanness of Jesus and (b) the real presence of Jesus in the Church. Only on the basis of these instances of real presence will the real presence of Jesus in the eucharist make sense."[35]

This matches that theological understanding that, if we can divide for purposes of discussion, we cannot divide spiritually. The undergirding ground for Church and sacrament, as we have noted before, is found in what Father Osborne terms "the flow: Jesus-Church-eucharist" that gives us a contemporary understanding of "Jesus as the *primordial*, the Church as the basic sacrament and the eucharist as the sacrament of the presence of the risen Lord."[36]

THE EUCHARIST AS SACRIFICE

During the sixteenth-century family estrangement of the Reformation, one of the keenest of disputed questions concerned the nature of the Eucharist as a sacrifice. This was linked to another pressing issue about the relationship of God's grace to our good works or, simply put, could human beings do anything, no matter how heroically virtuous, that could merit God's grace when that grace was, in fact, his free and, therefore, unearned and beyond earning, gift to men and women? The reformers of that period thought, perhaps mistakenly, that the Church taught that the Mass (the Eucharist) was a sacrifice of propitiation, or atonement, between humans and God, and that it undercut what was considered the single, unrepeatable, once and for all time, propitiatory sacrifice of Jesus on Calvary. This dispute centered first on belief about Jesus and secondarily on the Eucharist but it remains important to understand, not only for those interested in the family of the Church but for the Church in its ongoing ecumenical work of repairing relationships with the broader family of the Christian Churches.

In response to the question raised by reformers, the Council of Trent (1545) affirmed that at the very core of Church teaching was to be found the proposition that there was one, and one only, sacrifice of propitiation, that of Jesus. The bishops in council also held that everything, including our own good works, proceeds from God's grace and that, although we are not passive vessels but active agents in responding to God, our sinfulness made it impossible for us to effect the redemptive transactions of either reconciliation or justification. The Council stated that Jesus offered the sacrifice of himself once on Calvary in what they termed a "bloody" manner and that, in the Mass, the same sacrifice is represented in "an unbloody manner."

Centuries later, the ecumenical cooperation between the Christian Churches expresses this in a manner that offers a new theological basis for healing the family rift by speaking of the Mass as "a sacrament of the one sacrifice of Jesus."[37] Catholics believe, then, that expressing the relationship between the sacrifice of Jesus and the Eucharist as *sacrament* expresses "in a much better way, the Tridentine formulation: bloody/unbloody."[38]

Osborne expresses what the Church believes by saying of Jesus that "by his sacrifice he brought about the salvation of the world.... Jesus is the sacrament of God's justifying and saving love. Such a sacrament makes sense because there is the community (family) called Church which responds to this sacrificial message and reality of Jesus" and so becomes the "basic sacrament, and only on this foundation do we celebrate baptism and eucharist."[39]

The Eucharist is at the center of the Church Family's understanding of God's saving ways, the presence of the Risen Lord in the Church, and fully and truly in his humanness in the Eucharist.

RECONCILIATION

The Catholic family understands this sacrament as that ritual of the community or family in which, under the leadership of bishop or priest, "sinners are reconciled both to God and to the Church."[40] Catholics believe that the Church has the authority, through its institution by Christ, to identify, to isolate and, as it is said, to mitigate sin.

Some lifelong Catholics, accustomed to the practice of individual confession through a screen in a veiled booth, are surprised to learn that this was not the original practice of the Church, that, in fact, there was no specified ritual until A.D. 150. Reconciliation was a family matter, a function of Christian community life, ordinarily administered only once, when a person was near death. Only a thousand and more years later did it became a private exchange between priest and penitent under the influence of Irish monks as they developed a form of intense personal spiritual direction. Indeed, penance, or confession, as this sacrament has been variously termed, took on a culturally insistent and often severe mode through the influence of a spiritual extremist group called the Jansenists who were the first to emphasize the frequent use of the sacrament, the intense, often obsessive, and frequently disordering, examination of self for the smallest of imperfections that distorted its meaning and made its practice a heavy burden for many.

The liturgical renewal of Vatican II has restored a sense of the communal aspect of reconciliation that recognizes the social nature of many of our failures and therefore presents the reconciliation as one not carried out with an anonymous Divinity but with the community of the Church, of which Christ is the originating sacrament and in which he is present. According to Vatican II, the purpose of the sacrament is "to obtain pardon from the mercy of God" and to "be reconciled with the Church whom (sinners) have wounded by their sin and who, by its charity, its example and its prayer, collaborates in their conversion."[41] Being a sinner means that we have to learn to say that we are sorry. The Church family believes that its members, as in any family in which people hurt each other or become estranged, need reconciliation and that, in and through the family, because of Christ and God's free gift, it is made readily available to them.

Indeed, as McBrien emphasizes, the renewed rite of reconciliation stresses the effect of the sacrament as "reconciliation with God and with the Church. The minister functions more as a healer than a judge. Emphasis is placed on conversion inspired by the Church's proclamation of God's word."[42] This sacrament reveals what the Church preaches and what Catholics believe in a powerful way because it "reveals itself as the sacrament of God's mercy in the world, but also as a sinful community 'on the way' to the perfection of the Kingdom."[43]

Catholics believe that they must be sorry for their sins, be ready to confess them, receive absolution from God through the Church, and make satisfaction in some way, usually through carrying out a small penance of saying prayers or performing certain charitable acts, and that they must make every effort to overcome this sin in the future. This sacrament tells us, therefore, not only about God's nature but our own as well.

The notion of reconciling in and through the Church was expressed poignantly but pointedly by the late scholar of mythology, Joseph Campbell, who had seen, in his long lifetime, the Catholic Church into which he was baptized, regain the sense of the mytho-poetic language it had once forsaken in favor of a literal interpretation of many biblical statements. He asked, in a Honolulu hospital before his death in 1987, that a priest come to see him so that he could be reconciled "with the Church assembled." That wording captures a powerful sense of the relationship Catholics have with each other and to the family they constitute as the Church. The Church teaches that our sins can be forgiven in other ways, as in the reception of the Eucharist, but that a sacrament also exists that underscores that, if we never sin without some social impact, we are not alone in seeking and obtaining reconciliation with our family in faith and with God who is present in it.

We learn more about the theology of the Church, this family, as we understand it as the setting of relationships, the moving and transforming intimacies in which we glimpse something of God's nature and grasp the meaning of the sacraments. For in Reconciliation, we understand Jesus as the *primordial sacrament* and the Church as the basic *sacrament of Reconciliation*, "indicating," as Father McBrien observes, "that in every ecclesial activity [Christ] is present."[44] Questions about the ritual of reconciliation follow from that understanding of the Church. In

Vatican II, the Church restored a form of communal reconciliation as that which best reflects the experience of the early Church as well as the social context of human sin. It remains one of the ritual forms in which, in the context of the Church at prayer, men and women may examine their consciences, participate in the prayer of absolution and the following prayer of praise and blessing. The Sacrament of Reconciliation may be received this way as well as in the individual confession of one's sins to a priest.

MARRIAGE

The Sacrament of Marriage is celebrated by the man and woman who become husband and wife through it; they do so in close relationship to the Church that seals and witnesses it through the priest who presides and through the loving support it provides by its being a People of God and a loving human family at the same time. This sacrament, like the others, carries a history like that of a riverfront town that has marked centuries of flood levels on the gates and walls of its homes and buildings. For marriage has been looked at now this way and now that and we must read this history if we are to understand its richness, its scars and its recovery and restoration as a profound Mystery in whose intimacy men and women celebrate a love that participates in the work of creation and reveals the nature of Christ's relationship to his Church.

No small Mystery here, we might truly say, in looking back only to the beginning of the last century we may see how canon law—the official, and since much revised, law of the Church—spoke of marriage in the language of property rights and regulated it as a contract. This is, of course, another example of the loss of spiritual meaning, of how the letter of the law kills when something as sacred as marriage is turned over in the legal rather than the theological or pastoral mind and heart.

Vatican II remedied this distortion by restoring the early Church's understanding of marriage as a covenant that mirrored that for which it served as a metaphor, the relationship between God and Israel and between Christ and his Church. Even some modern commentators inadvertently divide what they intend to unite by trying to explain the metaphor. The union of man and woman in a celebration of their love and the symbolization of the love of Jesus for his Church happens all at once, at the same time and not in layers. This Mystery is not of the measurements of its transepts but of the measureless transcendence of the Church. We cannot divide marriage and man and woman and Jesus and his Church without diminishing our sense of one or the other.

Thus to say that "a marriage between Christians is a sacrament is to say that it is a two-storied reality...[the] first story, the ordinary human story...announces and makes explicit the communion of life and love between a Christian man and woman [while]...a second story, the religious and symbolic story... announces and makes explicit...the communion of life and love between Christ and Christ's people, the Church."[45] This is certainly helpful for purposes of discussion, but it may lessen our capacity to grasp that this sacrament encompasses one Mystery. Drawing blueprints for a religious Mystery resembles rendering a flat Mercator projection of the world on the wall; we distort the elements and lose a feeling for the unity of the whole.

And the Mystery here is profound indeed because marriage is the metaphor of the spirit that gives us, better than anything else, a sense of God's passionate relationship with his sometime sinning Chosen People and Jesus' passionate relationship with his sometime sinful Church, the People of God. We understand, then, that marriage cannot be cheapened, as it is when it is reduced to property rites and prenuptial agreements, or when it is looked on, by timid rigorist commentators who reduce it by regarding it as a lesser choice than chastity, or, in an even worse proposition at one period in Church history, an exercise of lower aspects of personality as a cure for concupiscence.

All of these notions, held at certain times under the influence of partial views of God and human personality, are the expected harvest from fields sown with splintered seeds to represent a fractured humanity divided, as moral theologians once put it, into decent (*honestae*) and indecent (*inhonestae*) parts. The creation of these subdivisions of human personality into these better parts (the soul, the spirit) and lesser parts (the body, the flesh) misrepresented Christ's teachings, his relationship to the Church and the Church's relationship to us, as well as the flawed but unitary nature of human personality. As human persons we are not unstable amalgams but *one* being.

Thanks to the work of Vatican II, the Church has returned to a healthier sense of matrimony as this true Mystery that cannot be understood if we do not grasp the true character of human personality as that which flourishes only in the intimacy of relationships with others. This healthy understanding of the total response of persons to each other—with their whole being, all at once, sometimes harmoniously and sometimes less than that, but ever and always human—is critical if we are not to be cowed by misinterpretations and distortions that make people feel uneasy if not guilty about being human. We can appreciate the overlapping Mystery of man and woman and Christ and his Church.

Marriage invites people into that non-abstract intimacy of loving each other that is the sacrament of God's relationship to us and Christ's to the Church. This sacrament accepts none of the fault-ridden caricatures of personality while it accepts the imperfection of human personality, that created state that makes us capable of what we long for in human and divine friendship. The Church underscores what relationships demand, that we give all of ourselves to each other in married love, that we commit ourselves to faithfulness that includes but is not totally summed up in sexual fidelity and that involves us everyday in the Paschal Mystery of Incarnation, Death and Resurrection that expresses and reveals the sacramental nature of our lives together.

That is why Jesus astounded his hearers when he denounced the then-accepted practice of easy divorce by which a man could rid himself of a wife for such trivial reasons as a bad meal or an undusted house. Jesus condemns adultery because it breaks the bond of relationship between man and woman, making sacrilege of the sacrament that seals what it reveals of the interwoven and inseparable religious mysteries of our relationships with each other and with God.

VATICAN II AND MARRIAGE

This is also why the Church has always safeguarded marriage even as, in its restored theology, it tries to listen to and understand the problems people experience living as close to each other as Jesus does to his Church. It is also why, in Vatican II, it has revised its own vocabulary and pastoral practice so that they match better the teachings of Jesus and the experience of ordinary, imperfect human beings.

The Church abandoned the notion of a *legal contract* and *property rights* and adopted the term *covenant* to speak of this sacrament. No longer does it distort the integrity of one relationship that has many facets by insisting that the procreation of children is its first and defining purpose. The Church realizes, as Vatican II expresses it, that the mutual love of marriage is more than biological union and "involves the good of the whole person, and…can enrich the expressions of body and mind with unique dignity, ennobling these expressions as special ingredients and signs of the friendship distinctive of marriage…. [S]uch love pervades the whole of [the spouses'] lives."[46]

WHAT NEW CATHOLICS AND NON-CATHOLICS CAN EXPECT

The Church has always taught that Catholics should be married in the Church at a eucharistic liturgy that underscores the Church both as prayer and as a teacher in the sacrament. Witnesses should be present, one of whom, as bishop, priest or deacon, is the official witness of the Church to the couple who author the sacrament together. These rules were once enforced in pastoral practices that seemed punitive, controlling, and not helpful to the love and relationship that was being celebrated or to the families of the marrying couple. Many people trace hard feelings about the Church back to incidents that occurred in the context of their seeking to be married.

Following the lead of Pope John XXIII, the Church has put away the severity with which some officials once dealt with believers in favor of the "medicine of love," and donned again its gentle shepherd's robes in counseling and preparing people for the sacrament of marriage. Gone are the harsh and sometimes estranging attitudes that often demeaned and embarrassed Catholics if they sought, for example, permission to marry a non-Catholic. Retired are the promises, for example, that non-Catholics once had to make in writing that they would raise the children Catholic. Replacing it is a reaffirmation, by Catholic spouses, of their faith in Jesus Christ and their intention "to live my Catholic faith in the Catholic Church " and "to do all in my power to share with our children the faith I have received by having them baptized and brought up as Catholics." They can do this orally or in writing and they must inform their spouse that they are doing so.

The Church also understands that many other Christian Churches celebrate true sacramental marriages and, while dispensations from the usual canonical form were always available, it is now possible to receive them so that the ceremony may be conducted in other Christian Churches, an action once forbidden to Catholics who would incur serious penalties for doing so. Now non-Catholics may serve as witnesses in the bridal parties and Catholics may do the same at weddings of Protestant and other friends. This altered pastoral practice reflects the true family attitude of the Church and reflects the ecumenical progress that has been made so that Catholics now recognize the sacramentality of Anglican and Lutheran marriages.

These approaches represent better the fact, as McBrien expresses it, that in matrimony the Church "reveals itself as the bride of Christ, as the sign that God is irrevocably committed to the human community in and through Christ.... [It is] a sign that the Church is a community of love brought about by the Holy Spirit... [that the] *family* is the most basic level of the Church's coming to life."[47]

WHAT THE FAMILY BELIEVES ABOUT DIVORCE

The Catholic Church has always taught that sacramental marriage is indissoluble, except by death. Nor does the Church grant divorces in the civil sense that abrogates marriages that have truly existed. The Church grants *annulments* that are official declarations, after investigations and through the processes of the Church courts, that a canonically valid marriage never existed between a particular man and woman. This does not deny their relationship or their love, the existence of a marriage or the legitimacy of children born from it. These marriages are judged not to have been canonically valid for one of many impediments or what are understood as consensual defects, for example, psychological states that render one of the persons incapable of giving full consent.

The Church, like a family that has grown wise through long historical experience, recognizes the complications and hazards of the human condition and has applied its insights in granting annulments to many couples who could demonstrate the presence of these impediments or defects. In the United States, for example, the late John Cardinal Cody of Chicago, invested generously in the archdiocesan marriage court so that petitions could be carefully examined and decisions could be made to free people from extremely painful and estranging circumstances. Dr. Leroy Wauck, psychological consultant to the Chicago archdiocesan court, offers examples of many couples who met on a weekend in World War II, were married right away and separated for many months while one spouse was overseas. After the war, they sometimes found that they were strangers to each other who nonetheless bore the burden of loveless but seemingly valid marriages for many years. The Church found that in many of these cases these people had not, because of the presence of a range of defects, entered valid marriages and were therefore eligible for the annulments that the Church understood were appropriate in such circumstances.

The family of the Church has also broadened and deepened its pastoral concern and care for the divorced and remarried. The Church family makes room now for those who ended canonically valid marriages with civil divorces even though it cannot grant them a decree of annulment. This concern for divorced Catholics who are in second marriages that are stable and sound is one of the compassionate developments that have flowed from the work of Vatican Council II. There are strong theological opinions that a Catholic, who, as Father McBrien puts it, "after prayerful consultation, has decided to remarry, may...be readmitted to the Church's sacramental life, assuming that no grave scandal is involved."[48]

Nowhere does the Church reveal its family nature more fully than in its pastoral dealings with sinners, the troubled and the discouraged, in short, the great parade in which we all march through life everyday.

WHAT THE FAMILY BELIEVES ABOUT SIN

Every member of every family, especially of the happy families whose likeness to each other Tolstoy observed, knows what is wrong with every other member of the family. Yet this knowledge, that can be used to strike sparks between siblings in a thousand moves and taunts that may carry over into adult life, does not destroy their relationships as much as it describes the way, trailing shortcomings like a wagon behind us, we may fall short of being grown up and yet measure up as loyal and loving brothers and sisters, sons and daughters, at the same time. If there is one thing that happy families grasp, it is their own imperfection, their members' capacity to irritate, to hurt, to be consistent as much in their faults as in their virtues, and yet to love, forgive, and support each other at the crucial and defining moments of life.

We might say, in a truly Catholic and profoundly human sense—and these are rivers that flow into each other from the same source—a family is only happy because it is imperfect. If parents and children were perfect, there would be no need for the love through which each respects and forgives the other for being human. "Earth's the right place for love," poet Robert Frost tells us, "I don't know where it's likely to go better."[49] Love may give us hints of Heaven but its natural home is earth, and that's where happy families are found. In the great myths that track our human story, it is always where we stumble and fall that we discover the gold.

The loving family is well acquainted with the pains and wonders of being human and, sooner or later, its members sample every kind of calamity that flows out of the breaks in this condition. The family breathes in and out through the relationships of its members and its glory arises from their ability—given to all lovers—to see rather than to be blind to each other's failures as well as each other's possibilities. The family that does not know what sin is cannot be a happy family. That is why, each in its own way, unhappy families eat away ignorantly at the bonds that bear the nourishment of affection. They are unhappy, not because they sin but because they do not understand imperfection and, therefore, can never really enter fully into life, but bicker at the entrance and bar the door to each other and to the growth that they could otherwise confer on each other.

Happy families are well acquainted with sinfulness but their attitude is never to condemn the sinner—the one who rejects relationship with them and with God—but, as with God and with the Catholic Church—to be ready to receive the wanderer back into its warm and well-lighted circle. Doing something really evil—and, indeed, doing anything really good—requires a robustness of personality, a knowingness and a willingness to accept the risks that takes sinning out of the category of imperfection. Loving and sinning are never small, distracted activities that leave no marks on ourselves or on others. Families can understand virtue and sin because they are both functions of the way we respond in our relationships with each other, that best test and expression of our relationship with God.

Sin deliberately forsakes relationship, it breaks a bond and the fibers of faith and hope that hold it together. Sin betrays relationship by *shattering* the trust that is its bedrock. It attacks the relationships we have within the extended human family, thereby breaking our covenant, as it is called, with God who parents us all. The "first understanding of sin in the Bible," McBrien tells us, "is 'to miss the mark.' To sin is to fail to achieve one's goal or to fail to measure up to one's highest standards...sin is *infidelity to the covenantal relationship* between God and ourselves."[50] We could never understand what that means unless we have had an experience of family life.

But that same experience—of how destructive our falsification or withdrawal of love can be—is also associated in family life with the idea of forgiveness. It is the unhappy family—the one manacled by the effects of sin—that is trapped by its inability to understand or to forgive that confronts us with the ruin that sin makes of relationships. That is what makes it unhappy in its own way.

The Church as a family understands sin and, if it condemns it, it stands always ready to forgive the sinner. Indeed, Jesus speaks of sin almost always in connection with forgiveness, the way happy families do and the way that the big family of the Church does. We really understand what Jesus teaches only because we have experienced the readiness to forgive and to make room for the estranged member in a loving family. We find our own story in that of the prodigal son, who has broken relationships with his family, squandered his inheritance in a far country, but who come home to be greeted by a father who embraces him, calls for a feast for which he kills the fatted calf. It is not the flock but the one lost sheep that the Good Shepherd seeks and rejoices at finding.

To become or to be a Catholic means to understand sin and to be ready to forgive it and to make room for the sinner, to be ever ready to love deeply enough to heal the relationship damaged by the prodigal sinner—a role we all play in small or large ways—that makes the Church the home of sinners, for whom a feast is always ready, and that makes it like every other happy family.

HOLY ORDERS

This sacrament identifies and imprints a lasting character on those who are called from the family of the Church to minister to the whole family of believers. As with the other sacraments, Holy Orders must be understood in terms of relationships, in the context of the community that is the People of God. It embraces three familiar and familial ministries within it, those of the bishop, the priest and the deacon. The family believes that "Holy Orders is a divinely instituted structure of the Church of Christ...(through which) the candidate is united with the ministry of Jesus and the apostolic Church and empowered to minister in the name and power of Christ in the Church and in the world."[51]

In families with the best-kept records, however, there is often uncertainty as to why it did this or that—coming to America, for example, or moving from one place to another—at certain highly significant choice points in its history. Similar uncertainty is found in the story of how Holy Orders first developed out of a sense of the Levitical ministry of the Old Testament in which we read of a priesthood of "the order of Melchisedech" that is probably the source of the word *Order* and that is applied in a variety of popular and theological reflections on the priesthood to this very day.

Still, many issues remain unresolved and those who are interested in the Church are often surprised, as are cradle Catholics, to learn the word *hieros*, priest, is applied only to Jesus in the New Testament and that ordinary Christians, considered in relationship to each other in the collective, or family sense, were referred to as priests. They are even more surprised to learn that it was not until 1208 that the family of the Church made an official declaration that priestly ministry is necessary to celebrate the Eucharist. In its social and psychological history, just as in those of families, learning and increased education have modified our understanding of how Holy Orders has been exercised in the context of ministry to the spiritual needs of the People of God.

A SHIFT TO THE INDIVIDUAL

As McBrien summarizes the matter, our image of the priesthood "is really a fusion of several different roles: disciple, apostle, presbyter-bishop, and eucharistic presider" and that this emerged "after the definitive separation from Judaism and the gradual growth in the sacrificial understanding of the Eucharist."[52] The ministerial calling, along with many others, such as those of the physician and the lawyer, expressed the core of their followers' identity in widely, and sometimes wildly, different ways, as they donned the vesture, or entered the maze, of the transforming dynamics of culture throughout history.

We know, for example, that, in the early Church, those who presided at the Eucharist did so with the agreement of the

community but that "we don't know how and why certain figures presided at first." By the second century, we do know that
"only the bishop and his appointees presided."[53] By the next
century we know that candidates entered the ministry of bishop,
presbyter and deacon through ordination.[54] We also understand
that, in the Middle Ages, the powerful feudal culture melded
these ministerial offices into the royal line, endowing them with
the sense of power, privilege, and the court dress that survives in
the rings, chains, crowns, thrones and other robes and customs
still associated with the bishopric and the priesthood.

The family history also tells us that in reaction to the damaging rift of the Reformation in which the need for ministers to
celebrate the Eucharist was challenged on the basis that Christ's
one-time sacrifice sufficed and needed no repetition on later
altars, the Council of Trent (1545) affirmed the sacrificial
priesthood, its place in the culturally absorbed hierarchical culture and, in a move that affected the priesthood well into the
last century, emphasized the *personal* and *private* nature of being
a priest, giving it an individualistic emphasis that tore it out of
the context of family relationships. The *monastic* model of the
priest, pursuing a life outside the broader family of the Church,
was also introduced with its marked emphasis on the priesthood
as a *state in life*, and a superior one at that, rather than a *ministry*
that recognized the meaning of the priesthood in the service of
the community. *Celibacy*, the vow not to marry, is a discipline of
the Church rather than an essential note of the sacrament of
Holy Orders. It was imposed only on priests of the Latin rite in

the twelfth century, at least partially to block priests from passing on Church lands to their heirs.

It was not until Vatican II that a beginning was made to restore a sense of Holy Orders as embracing the ministry of the bishop that is shared with priest and deacon. Understanding the Church as a People of God, a big family, it accepted the special priesthood of the ordained while it refreshed the traditional notion of the participation of the laity in the priesthood of Jesus. The ministry of bishops was also addressed, reviving their *collegial* relationship, mirroring that of the college of the apostles, a relationship that united them with each other and with the pope as the bishop of Rome. This principle of collegiality was applied as well to the priesthood and to the entire Church and the range of ministerial relationships was also restored by the return of the permanent diaconate.

The Catholic family recognizes that Holy Orders encompasses the three-fold ministry of bishop-priest-deacon in relationship to the Church as the People of God. That is the context of the Catholic understanding of this sacrament and is the basis for the ecumenical research that continues between the Christian Churches in their effort to bring about a family reunion of belief and recognition of their common inheritance.

The crisis occasioned in 2001 by the sex abuse scandal exposed the problematic nature of a priesthood frozen as a state of life in a rigid cultural form when it can only express itself and flourish in the healthy relationships of service to the family of the Church. As a result of this scandal, one of the most serious the Church has suffered, the Church is digging through the cultural rubble that has obscured and put at risk the sacramental calling of the priesthood. The Catholic family grieves for this system failure and is working to restore the priesthood to the healthy context of ministry. It understands that, at the very center of Catholic belief, is a realization that the "sacramental reality of the Church is expressed in the sacrament of Holy Order, and through it, Jesus, our High Priest, continues to minister on our behalf."[55]

ANOINTING OF THE SICK

The Catholic family understands that this sacrament, ordinarily called, as many older Catholics remember, by titles in which one could hear the sirens and see the lights of emergency vehicles, *Extreme Unction* and the *Last Rites*. Yet the meaning of this sacrament is not found in these notions nor is its sense that the family never leaves anybody out, that it seeks out and calls back from isolation those members who are ill or debilitated in one way or the other. It is a sacrament of relationship, joining the whole community—the young and vigorous with the older and even the ill—in a family picture in which we read their love for each other and through which, with the Church, they pray for and support each other.

It is understood, therefore, in the context of ministry to the family and defined as "one ritual component of a more extensive ensemble of ritual prayer that is part of the Church's pastoral care for the seriously sick and/or the dying...the reformed rite restored the more traditional (premedieval) perspective on the sacrament as the ordinary rite for the strengthening of those whose health is debilitated by physical illness or old age. This change of perspective has been well received by the faithful."[56]

THE FAMILY AS A SACRAMENT

In an extended sense, we may see the family of the Church as a sacrament because we understand that it carries out, in its utterly human yet completely adequate way, the work of the Church as a sacrament. The family, along with its beliefs and practices, is rooted in Jesus and reveals him to its own members and to the world at large.

The sacraments are sacred signs but they are communicated by human beings in profoundly human ways. The Church as a big family has, we might say, a feel for the sacramental nature of creation and reflects it in its every unself-conscious and self-forgetting activity.

Would you like to be a Catholic? You would not be joining an army but a family, not a monarchy but a community in which the principles of sacramentality are displayed, honored and shared every day. What is that principle, so ordered to life and honor, justice and love, every day? It is, as McBrien summarizes it, "the notion that all reality, both animate and inanimate, is potentially or in fact the bearer of God's presence and the instrument of God's saving activity on humanity's behalf."[57]

Any man or woman interested in the Church learns that the sacraments contain everything they must understand about it.

Its *sacramentality* is rooted "in the nature of a sacrament, i.e., a visible sign of the invisible presence and activity of God."[58] This is linked to the other defining principles, that of *mediation*, God's working through secondary agents to accomplish his work, and *community*, that "the end of all God's activity is the union of humanity" so that sacramentality represents "one of the central theological characteristics of Catholicism."[59]

People who enter the Church do not feel that they are entering a foreign country where no one speaks their language. The language of the family is sacramental, concerns the things in life that are of concern to every human person, celebrates not escape from the world, but entrance fully into it. They feel they have met this family before, that all of this is familiar, that it fits their deepest spiritual longings and human needs for friendship and love. They will feel that the entrance is not guarded by mythical flame-bearing figures but that the door is opened by someone like Blessed Pope John XXIII who, on his first night as pope, spoke to the crowds of how *everything* in life, *everything* bears God's mark and message. And they will hear his welcome in the name of the Lord in his reply, perhaps the most Catholic sentence of the twentieth century, when asked why he had convened Vatican Council II, "To make the human sojourn on earth less sad."

[1] Richard T. McBrien, ed., *The HarperCollins Encyclopedia of Catholicism* (New York: HarperCollins, 1995), p. 985.

[2] McBrien, *Encyclopedia*, p. 359.

[3] *American Heritage Dictionary* (New York: Delta, 1994).

[4] Quoted in McBrien, *Encyclopedia*, loc. cit.

[5] William James, *The Varieties of Religious Experience* (New York: Vintage Books/Library of America, 1990), lecture 2.

[6] McBrien, *Encyclopedia*, p. 364.

[7] Gordon Willard Allport, *The Individual and His Religion: A Psychological Interpretation* (New York: Macmillan, 1967).

[8] *American Heritage Dictionary*, op. cit.

[9] John L. McKenzie, *Dictionary of the Bible* (New York: Macmillan, 1965), pp. 135, 136.

[10] McKenzie, p. 273.

[11] McBrien, *Encyclopedia*, p. 314.

[12] Ibid.

[13] See McBrien, *Encyclopedia*, p. 118.

[14] McBrien, *Catholicism* (New York: HarperCollins, 1994), p. 679.

[15] McBrien, *Encyclopedia*, p. 457.

[16] Nancy Dallavalle, quoted in McBrien, *Encyclopedia*, p. 900.

[17] Mark A. Francis, quoted in McBrien, *Encyclopedia*, p. 1146.

[18] Ibid.

[19] Quoted in Dallaville, loc. cit.

[20] *Vatican Council II: The Basic Sixteen Documents, Lumen Gentium*, ed. by Austin Flannery, O.P. (Northport, NY: Costello Publishing Co. 1996), n. 1, n. 9, n. 48.

21 *American Heritage Dictionary*, op. cit.

22 Leo Tolstoy, *Anna Karenina* (New York: Random House, 1965), Part Two, Ch. 1.

23 McBrien, *Catholicism*, p. 791.

24 Ibid.

25 Kenan B. Osborne, *Christian Sacraments in a Postmodern World: A Theology for the Third Millennium* (New York: Paulist Press, 2000), p. 85.

26 Ibid., pp. 86, 87.

27 Ibid., p. 90.

28 Regis A. Duffy, quoted in McBrien, *Encyclopedia*, p. 481.

29 Ibid.

30 Duffy, quoted in McBrien, *Encyclopedia*, p. 484.

31 Joseph Campbell, *Thou Art That: Transforming Religious Metaphor*, Eugene Kennedy, ed. (Novato, Calif.: New World Library, 2001), p. 6.

32 See Duffy, loc. cit.

33 Kenan B. Osborne, *The Christian Sacraments of Initiation: Baptism, Confirmation, Eucharist* (New York: Paulist Press, 1998), p. 169.

34 Ibid.

35 Ibid., p. 210.

36 Ibid., p. 189.

37 Ibid., p. 224.

38 Ibid.

39 Op. cit., p. 225.

40 McBrien, *Encyclopedia*, p. 1083.

[41] *Vatican Council II: The Basic Sixteen Documents, Lumen Gentium*, n. 11.

[42] McBrien, *Catholicism*, pp. 841, 842.

[43] Ibid.

[44] McBrien, *Encyclopedia*, p. 1086.

[45] Michael G. Lawler in *Encyclopedia*, p. 824.

[46] *Vatican Council II: The Basic Sixteen Documents, Pastoral Constitution on the Church in the Modern World*, n. 49.

[47] McBrien, *Catholicism*, p. 863.

[48] McBrien, *Catholicism*, p. 862.

[49] Robert Frost, *Birches* (New York: Henry Holt, 1990).

[50] McBrien, *Catholicism*, pp. 952, 953.

[51] Frederick J. Cwiekowski in *Encyclopedia*, p. 620.

[52] McBrien, *Catholicism*, p. 878.

[53] Ibid., p. 878.

[54] Ibid., p. 879.

[55] McBrien, *Catholicism*, p. 879.

[56] Andrew D. Ciferni, quoted in McBrien, *Encyclopedia*, p. 57.

[57] McBrien, *Encyclopedia*, p. 1148.

[58] Ibid.

[59] Ibid.